D1624566

Fragments of War

Fragments of War

•

A Marine's Personal Journey

•

BERTRAM A. YAFFE

NAVAL INSTITUTE PRESS
Annapolis, Maryland

Library of Congress Cataloging-in-Publication Data

Yaffe, Bertram A., 1920–

      Fragments of War: a marine's personal journey / Bertram A. Yaffe.

         p.   cm.

      ISBN 1-55750-979-4 (alk. paper)

      1. Yaffe, Bertram A., 1920– . 2. World War, 1939–1945—Campaigns— Pacific Area. 3. World War, 1939–1945—Personal narratives, American. 4. United States. Marine Corps—Biography. 5. Soliders—United States—Biography. I. Title.

D767.9.Y34 1999

940.54'25—dc21   98-53483

[B]

Printed in the United States of America on acid-free paper ∞

06 05 04 03 02 01 00 99   9 8 7 6 5 4 3 2

First printing

Contents

Preface

Among the Americans who served on Iwo Island uncommon valor was a common virtue.

Adm. Chester W. Nimitz, 1945

So long as [we] propose . . . no *moral equivalent* of war . . . so long [do we] fail to realize the full inwardness of the situation. . . . All of the qualities of a man acquire dignity when he knows that the service of the collectivity that owns him needs them. If proud of the collectivity, his own pride rises in proportion. . . . I spoke of the "moral equivalent" of war. So far, war has been the only force that can discipline a whole community. . . . But I have no serious doubt that the ordinary prides and shames of social man, once developed to a certain intensity, are capable of organizing such a moral equivalent as I have sketched. . . . It is but a question of time . . . and of opinion-making men seizing historic opportunities.

William James, "The Moral Equivalent of War"

Nearly two years ago, while engaged in the ongoing, Sisyphean task of discarding a half-century's accumulation of assorted papers, artifacts, memorabilia, and just plain junk, I opened a seabag that a very young Marine Corps officer had carried on his return from the South Pacific in April of 1945. I am sure that at some point I went through its contents, but I did not recollect doing so.

Carelessly crushed among many remarkably ordinary things was a document titled "Special Action Report: 3d Tank Battalion," a confidential account of the battalion's role in the Battle of Iwo Jima. As the Bn-3, the unit's operations officer, I had written it immediately after the campaign, drawing on daily diaries that my staff and I kept during the action. Knowing that on my return I would be assigned as operations officer of the Camp Pendleton Tank Training School in Oceanside, California, I had requested permission to take a copy of the report as a "training tool." As I retrieved the document from the seabag, I saw it only as a fragment of memorabilia. I realize now, however, that it was the catalytic fragment that impelled the writing of this memoir.

Like so many World War II veterans in 1946, I was eager to get on with a life outside the military. Perhaps too hastily, I buried associations and memories that were pivotal in forging my view of reality, but—as William James, a psychologist as well as a philosopher, recognized—you cannot neatly separate events from the full inwardness of the situation.

In January of 1993, some months after digesting the Special Action Report as though I were reading it for the first time, I attended the inauguration of President Clinton. The evening before the ceremony, I was enjoying dinner with some members of the Washington Press Corps—E. J. Dionne (*Washington Post*) and Joe Klein (*Newsweek*) among others—clearly a group a full generation removed from me. E. J. had been an integral part of my 1970 campaign for the Tenth U.S. Congressional District seat from Massachusetts. During the evening, E. J. and I offhandedly referred to the obligatory insertion of the phrase "decorated Marine Corps veteran" in the leads for our campaign press releases. The conversation took a serious turn when several of those present expressed some anxiety that we were moving, however inevitably, into an era when our leaders would no longer have been shaped by the World War II experience. I was surprised, indeed affected, by the depth of their concern and respect for an epoch that many of their generation had considered with irreverence, almost impatience, twenty-five years previously. Their obvious and sincere awe with regard to the significance of that period enhanced my determination to come to terms with the experience as well as the intensity of my personal response to it.

These pages are the result of that determination. Writing this book has also greatly enhanced my appreciation not only of the relevancy and urgency of James's call for the "moral equivalent" of war but also of the individual need to identify with that larger "collectivity" that owns and needs us. I gratefully acknowledge the marines of Baker Company, 3d Tank Battalion, 3d Marine Division, who have generously opened their memories—treasured and some most painful—to help me reconstruct much of what follows. Tom Murphy is a virtual repository of lore and is also the beloved, unofficial historian of B Company. Lou Spiller, Tom Hughes, Frank Rawcliffe, Bob Riebe, and Paul Ryan have been most responsive and eager to help me keep the facts straight. They are members of a cadre who always fondly greet one another with "Hey, you brought us back alive." Though said laughingly, it asserts a mutual love among men who entrusted their lives to one another.

Many of the fragments used as the chapter epigraphs express ideas that I formed in some cases years after the experiences that triggered them. I came upon the statement by Viktor Frankl that I quote at the opening of chapter 1, for instance, some twenty years after the war. It was particularly meaningful to me because he was writing *Man's Search for Meaning* at the same time that the young author of the present memoir was grasping around the edges of that same fragment of thought—with the difference that Frankl's circumstances were incomparably more horrifying than mine. At that time he was in a Nazi concentration camp, while I was with a battalion of which I was immensely proud.

I half-apologize for including the two Bronze Star commendations as "fragments." They are, of course, far from Silver Stars and Navy Crosses, and I am well aware that many who served are at least as deserving as I but did not receive commendations. The awards have become important to me as fragments for points-of-departure in my effort to understand that marine in his early twenties who, although he shares my name, is sometimes difficult for me to recognize. He is much more probing and confident in his conclusions than I have become, and he is impatient with my tendency to tolerate equivocations and inequities in a complex world.

The young marine's persistence in trying "to grasp reality" was not entirely unavailing. I have never abandoned his idea that consciousness is a striving, indivisible process, one that invites, through a mind uncluttered, the silent question: what is the meaning of life? Most times, of course, I do not transcend the fragmentation of consciousness—or the clutter. Still, there are times during solitary contemplative interludes when the fragments—some precious, others painfully poignant—meld into an ineffable whole. I thank him for that.

Finally, I must share with the reader what I recognize to be the "Pirandello phenomenon." In his play *Six Characters in Search of an Author* Luigi Pirandello gives us a forceful story of six people who are waiting to burst into life. They will not be denied. "We want to live," says the father, "only for a moment . . . in you." In the writing and rewriting of this memoir, there were at least two such persons. One is a lone immigrant waif. The other is a beautiful, forever youthful woman who—despite our separation for nearly two and a half years while I was in the South Pacific and her premature death—continues to be present though absent.

ONE _The Silent Question_

From time to time, I seem to hear a question echoing out of the depths of stillness. But he who asks it does not know that he is asking it, and he to whom the question is addressed is not aware that he is being questioned. . . . This is the question: "Art thou, perhaps, the power that can help me. . . . to have faith in reality, in the verities of existence, so that life will afford some aim for me and existence will have some meaning[?] Who, indeed, can help me if thou canst not?"

Martin Buber, "The Silent Question"

Ultimately, man should not ask what the meaning of his life is, but rather must recognize that it is he who is asked. In a word, each man is questioned by life.

Viktor Frankl, _Man's Search for Meaning_

The fifteen minutes before 0830, 21 July 1944, are so deeply fused into my consciousness that they have become a defining point in my life. They kindled my reverence for the pulsating fact of life, and they altered me forever. The background events—historic, momentous, deafening as they were—have become secondary to a thought that unexpectedly insinuated itself (inappropriately, I felt at the time) into my mind.

On that date in 1944 I was commander of Baker Company, 3d Tank Battalion, 3d Marine Division. At 0800 I was in my tank on its individual landing craft, an LCM (landing craft, mechanized), the leading point in an echeloned myriad of craft headed toward the coral beaches and cliffs of Apra Harbor on the island of Guam in the Mariana Islands.

The previous month had witnessed a critical shift in World War II as the American armed forces took the offensive. On 6 June, General Eisenhower's army assaulted the beaches of Normandy and began the unshackling of a besieged Western Europe. In the Pacific, the U.S. fleet fought the awesome battle of the carriers as marines and soldiers discarded the pattern of island-hopping and took a thousand-mile leap into the enemy's strongly fortified lair to establish a base for strategic air power. Guam would be the first American-held territory to be recovered from the Japanese. But beyond the historical significance and the boosting of morale, the possession of Guam's airfields would allow American B-29s to reach Japan's crowded cities some twelve hundred miles away. The Japanese could not, did not, relinquish the Marianas meekly.

The original plan for the Battle of the Marianas called for a 15 June, D day assault on the island of Saipan and three days later, W day, a landing on Guam by the 3d Marine Division and the 1st Provisional Marine Brigade. In support of this operation, the U.S. Navy's Fifth Fleet assembled and uncoiled the most powerful armada the world had ever known. Things did not, however, go according to plan.

It later became evident that the Japanese had not anticipated an attack on Guam so soon. As the American strategy unfolded, Vice Admiral Ozawa, who had been preparing for an expected engagement nearer the Philippines, headed north toward Guam with his First Mobile Fleet and the assurance that for this, the decisive battle, he had at his disposal practically every remaining vessel in the Japanese Navy—carriers with combat planes, battleships, cruisers, and destroyers.

Immediately following the landing on Saipan, U.S. admiral Spruance became aware of this enemy threat as he was preparing for the invasion of Guam on 18 June. Realizing that he could not fight simultaneously a major naval battle and support the Guam operation, he directed all troop and tank carriers to safety. While the ensuing two-day sea battle on 19–20 June was devastating to the Japanese fleet, it was also very costly in planes and airmen to the Americans. The landing on Guam was delayed for a month—a time we spent in relative safety circling the Marshall Islands, which had been secured in winter 1944.

Baker Company, well-trained and fully briefed, was eager for the scheduled 18 June operation. I had been an integral part of the company since its formation at Camp Lejeune, North Carolina, in the summer of 1942 after my training at Quantico. Except for a ten-week detachment for tank tactics training with the U.S. Army at Fort Knox, B Company had been my home in the Marine Corps. Having served successively as a platoon leader, executive officer, and now company commander, I knew very well every one of the two hundred twenty marines in the company. For a while I even had the distasteful task of censoring their mail. And, of course, they knew me. Guam would not be our "baptism by fire"; we had participated in the defense of Guadalcanal and had landed and secured the beachhead at Empress Augusta Bay on Bougainville the previous November.

A month's delay in a major phase of an amphibious assault as well-planned and synchronized as the Marianas landings dulls the edges. Esprit de corps begins to dissipate, especially in the confined quarters of navy landing ships. For the Guam operation, the three companies of the 3d Tank Battalion were distributed among several LSDs (landing ships, dock). Company B was on the LSD *Gunston Hall*. An LSD is a U-shaped boat with a dry dock pocketed within the two horns of its configuration. Each LSD accommodates eighteen LCMs with a medium tank on each. For crews to load or disembark from the LCMs for combat, the aft gate of the LSD was opened, and the entering waters buoyed the smaller craft. The horns of the ship accommodated living quarters for the navy crewmen and the marines. The base of the U-shape was broadened to accommodate the ship's operational needs, officers' quarters, and a mess hall.

I had made it a point to brief the platoon leaders and tank commanders between 1000 and 1100 every morning before the scheduled landing. Now, with the delay, these briefings would be exercises in boredom. Previously we had turned over the engines of the tanks every day; in the present situation, however, it was necessary to alternate days in order to conserve fuel. The only semblance of a meaningful routine was the time devoted to calisthenics and the maintenance of vehicles and weapons to protect them against the corrosive effects of salt water and weather. Beyond these perfunctory chores and standing watch for enemy aircraft, the LSDs, LSTs (landing ships, tank), and troop carriers with the hovering destroyers were a flotilla of poker, pinochle, chess, and cribbage games.

The previous November, during the battle for the beachhead at Empress Augusta Bay, I had contracted a fungal infection around an insect bite on my right hand; the inflammation had now spread up my arm, neck, and face. Though the medicines available at the time (antiseptic dyes and salicylic acid) did little to rid me of the problem, the condition was tolerable as long as I had fresh air. I had also contracted malaria, a disease that occasioned chills and fevers as well as spells of prolonged nausea.

Aboard the LSD, the close quarters I shared with two navy officers were very humid, and my discomfort from the fungus intensified during the nights when personnel not on watch were not allowed on deck. When it became obvious that we would be aboard much longer than expected, the ship's captain suggested I take a sleeping bag and sleep in a designated area of the deck, weather permitting.

Those evening routines are very vivid in my memory. After chow, before dark, I would visit with the tank crews and other marines in Company B and share whatever scuttlebutt I had or could reasonably imagine. The informal encounters were helpful to me and, I felt, to them because there was no pretense that the boredom wasn't affecting morale. The most exciting news I brought to the men was that we had arranged to get mail on the two occasions when supply ships would make their deliveries.

Just before darkness I would return to the officers' mess for a game of chess or cribbage. Then I would read until the changing of the watch just before 2400. The captain asked that I go to the deck only during the change because there would be less chance of light escaping the hatches or causing confusion among the men on watch. The solitary nights on the deck of the *Gunston Hall,* where I was surrounded by the waves of the Pacific and the skies of the Southern Hemisphere, provided me a good time and a good place for contemplation.

Over the previous year and a half that I had been in the South Pacific, Erna, my wife, had worked assiduously to keep me supplied with books and periodicals. These—along with other volumes I had brought with me or acquired in the book stores of Auckland, New Zealand, during the six months of our staging there—afforded extensive reading in the matters that preoccupied me.

When we embarked for the operation for Guam, I selected three volumes: Julian Huxley's *Man in the Modern World,* a book of essays by Bertrand Russell entitled *Mysticism and Logic,* and almost as an afterthought, Henri Bergson's *Creative Evolution*. I had already read and wrestled with each of them and felt they were significant enough for me now to tackle from a different perspective. The word *perspective* Russell defines as "the assemblage of all . . . present objects of sense." I knew, from experience, that my own perspective was about to change. In combat, reality seems more intensely present than usual. It is not *there;* it is *here*.

Relaxing the grip of concentration on an assault that was now weeks away freed my thoughts, which then turned to the fact of life's existing at all. This was the object of my reverence, the focus of my contemplation.

Nobody knew how life began on earth nearly four billion years ago. Life, my intuition told me, was an offspring of the cosmic dancing among molecules and chemical systems that had reached certain thresholds of complexity. That life arose naturally did not diminish its mystery, its sacredness, or my reverence for the things nature could do in the fullness of time. Biologist Julian Huxley wrote that "mankind is evolution becoming aware of itself." His vision of life—pulsating, striving through billions of years and myriad organisms of increasing complexity to attain comprehension—inspired me to think that with awareness comes humanity and that with humanity comes the responsibility to try to contribute to the evolutionary process.

I made a distinction between the description and the understanding of cosmic phenomena. Describing evolution seemed like a materialist concern. Following fossils and fruit flies through their various mutations would give us a reasonable chart line from primeval protoplasm to the present. Materialism, however, struck me as reductionist, as not discerning Henry James's "figure in the carpet"—the fantastically complex, coherent, intimate organism that was life. As a young marine, I doubted that rational inquiry could fathom the ultimate reality behind the forces at work in evolution.

These were some of the thoughts that consumed me on those evenings of solitude. I also mulled over the irony of my fighting a war against the Imperial Japanese Army and tried to understand—assimilate—my recent combat encounters on the rain forest island of Bougainville.

Faced with fewer distractions I succumbed to the natural inclination to reconstruct the chain of events that had brought me to Guam. A critical link was forged by events, passions, and poignant choices going back to 1904, in the province of Lithuania in czarist Russia. From there began the solitary journey of an adolescent who sailed in steerage with an identification card around his neck written in a language he could not read.

There had been a precedent for the 1941 surprise assault on Pearl Harbor. On 8 February 1904 five flotillas of destroyers had been detached from the Japanese fleet for an unsuspected strike on the Russian Far East Squadron at Port Arthur, precipitating the Russo-Japanese War of 1904–5. There were, of course, political and economic reasons behind this war, mostly having to do with the rivalry between these nations in developing spheres of influence in the Far East, at the expense of China. During the hostilities between Japan and China at the turn of the century, Russia had occupied Manchuria.

For the Jews of Russia and its incorporated Grand Duchy of Lithuania, these larger origins of international conflict were dwarfed by brutal day-to-day living conditions. In *A Century of Ambivalence* Zvi Gitelman gives a compelling description of one aspect of this discrimination:

during the thirty years of Nicholas's rule . . . the harshest decree was issued in 1827 when the tsar ordered that each Jewish community deliver up a quota of military recruits. Jews were to serve for twenty-five years in the military, beginning at age eighteen, but the draftable age was as low as twelve. Those under eighteen would serve in special units called Cantonist battalions until they reached eighteen, whereupon they would begin their regular quarter century of service. As if a term of army service of thirty years or more were not enough, strenuous efforts were made to convert the recruits to Russian Orthodoxy. . . . A double catastrophe fell on the heads of Russian Jewry: their sons would be taken away not only from their homes and families, but in all likelihood also from their religion. . . . Alexander Herzen described the scene as 'one of the most awful sights I have ever seen. . . . Pale, exhausted, with frightened faces, they stood in thick, clumsy, soldiers' overcoats . . . fixing helpless, pitiful eyes on the garrison, soldiers who were roughly getting them into ranks. The white lips, the blue rings under their eyes bore witness to fever or chill. And these sick children, without care or kindness, exposed to the raw wind that blows unobstructed from the Arctic Ocean, were going to their graves.' Little wonder that all sorts of subterfuges were used in attempts to avoid military service.

In retrospect, it is difficult to separate the fragments that my inquisitiveness extracted from my father as I was growing up in Sparta, Georgia, from later archival inquiries about his generation of immigrants. Sparta was a town in the dead center of a moribund stretch of cotton fields populated by struggling sharecroppers, mostly blacks, and shopkeepers living on the fringe of financial failure, about thirty miles from the infamous Tobacco Road. On those nights in the South Pacific I wondered how my father got there and I got here.

In *World of Our Fathers* Irving Howe writes that while there were significant differences among the experiences of immigrant Jews, "what is shown here regarding the immigrants of the East Side of New York also holds for those in other large cities. As for the relatively small number of Jews who settled in small towns or became farmers, that is another story." Louis Yaffe's is another story.

. . .

"Happy birthday!" my father called to me as I veered from my friends to drop my books off at our store. He had a soft, Yiddish Southern drawl. Then as an afterthought, only obliquely meant for me: "Soon after I was your age, I had to leave."

I think I had heard the story before, but it had not registered. I knew him better now. Besides, I was thirteen and I was supposed to ask questions. We were standing in the warm Georgia sunshine in front of Louis Yaffe's General Merchandise Store.

"Why? Why did you have to leave?"

"My mother. The Russian Army would force every other young Jew in the family into the camps. They would keep you for twenty-five years. Between the army and the Cossacks, things had always been bad, but when the Japanese started that war, it was certain that I was the one to go into the camps. Two of my brothers had gone to Vilna. They were much older and were, like you say, 'radical.' There was another brother, a little older than me, who was very smart and the *shtetl*—the village—sent him to study at a Yeshiva, like an advanced school.

"I had an older sister who had gone to America with her husband, and my father had always planned on me coming here when I finished my schooling. Education was very important to him, but the draft was closing in on me. And my mother could not stand for me to be taken in the czar's army. There was a farm in Poland where the young boys could work until they had enough money to go to America. Finally things got so bad they gave me ten dollars to keep and hide until it was time to leave with a family that took me to the farm." The ten dollars reminded him of something: he handed me two dollars for my birthday.

I think I asked him only two other questions before I pocketed the money and joined my friends, who were waiting impatiently for me to get my glove and baseball from inside the store. "How old were you when you came to America?"

"Not quite sixteen."

"By yourself?"

He nodded. "Your friends are waiting," he then reminded me. I can guess at some of the factors that caused him to leave New York after only a few weeks: nostalgia for the small Russian villages he had left behind and an aversion to the teeming, tenemented throngs around him—an aversion mixed, perhaps, with a wistful loneliness among so many who, however destitute, were sustained by strong family ties. Mostly, I suspect, it was a spirit of independence that drove him south, where he joined a stable of Jewish youths peddling merchandise from horse and wagon throughout the Georgia countryside for the wholesalers in Augusta. Later, to all who knew him, this streak of independence was recognized as a signature, ingrained stubbornness.

Other immigrants went south as whole families, staking out towns and small cities to become merchants. Among these, Nathan and Ethel Sperling migrated to South Carolina, then to Augusta, and finally to Waynesboro, Georgia. There they established a store that prospered, and they nurtured a family of five daughters and two sons.

"Your mother was beautiful." That statement always came with a gaze into the distance as he summoned the revered image. She died when I was two years old, a tragic event of enduring significance in our lives, and most of my inquiries about it brought forth only the barest of responses from him.

I persisted despite the wall of gloom he usually built around himself when the subject came up. On one of these occasions, when I was reading him the front page of the Atlanta *Journal*— I was only nine or ten years old, but he was illiterate—my power-through-literacy emboldened me to strike through his melancholia. "I know," I said. I think of the yellowing photograph on the mantle in his room. "Everyone says so. But how did you meet her?"

"I used to stop at the Sperlings' store to fill in merchandise on my wagon rather than go back to Augusta. Poppa Sperling didn't like that. But Mother and the girls ran the store while he mostly read the Talmud. Fannie and her sisters insisted on helping me and some of the other peddlers who were my friends." He would brighten up a bit with the memory.

It was easy to understand why "Mother and the girls" encouraged the young peddlers to stop at the store. These young women would never marry out of their heritage and the "traveling boys" were obvious candidates for brightening their routine of work and rigorous study. Education and minding the store were articles of faith for these women. Fannie was next to the oldest, and the photograph did indeed reflect her beauty—and her strength. It was also easy to understand her attraction to the handsome, generally carefree, and rootless Louis, whose aspiration for independence and self-reliance was circumscribed by limited education. These Sperling women would take care of that, though.

Louis and Fannie were married in 1913, the year Henry Ford announced that within one year he would produce "one million cars to be available for all Americans." The days of the Southern Jewish peddlers were numbered. The young men and their wives scrambled to open stores in the various small cities and towns scattered through the cotton fields of Georgia.

The next seven years were good ones for my parents as they established a successful business, largely owing to their affable personalities—the educated, vivacious Fannie and her adoring husband. The store prospered, and they built a home for themselves as the family grew with the births of three children: my sister, Rosa; my brother, Carl; and finally, in 1920, me.

Then in 1922 Louis Yaffe's world began to fall apart. Young Carl died of a sarcoma soon after they moved into their new home, and Fannie, our mother, died of leukemia a year later. Louis was left with a young daughter, a son just out of infancy, and a store that had largely depended on the managerial skills of Fannie—all in a culture that he was coming only haltingly to comprehend. And the Great Depression was yet to come.

Despite the bleakness of the situation, I do not remember these early years with any pain. My nurturing came mostly from Aunt Emma, a large black housekeeper whose innate good humor and constant concern for my welfare quickly established her as more than a nursemaid. Well-meaning neighbors and friends—all white—deferred to Emma where I was concerned. That relieved our father from a role he was not equipped to assume. His tutorship would wait until I was five or six years old, when he would sit me on an elevated stool and teach me to run the cash register in the store.

With Rosa the situation was different and difficult. Her memories of our mother and brother were more vivid than mine, and her sense of abandonment was acute. Although Louis had left his Lithuanian village at an early age, the shtetl's rigid attitude concerning the role of young women was never erased from his mind. My father was frustrated over a contradiction: he could not tolerate the same independence of spirit in his daughter that he had found to be so magnetic in his beloved wife. The frustration became a source of dissension, and Rosa's personal satisfaction during adolescence was confined to her scholastic attainments, which were outstanding.

By 1931, when the depth of depression came—accompanied by the successive failures of Sparta's small banks—Louis had developed an aptitude for survival. Among the small merchants of Sparta and the populace of the county, black and white, there developed an economy, not uncommon throughout the rural areas of the South, based on credit, mutual trust, and frequent bartering of goods and services. He became a respected member of that community. Indeed, he had found his shtetl in Sparta.

Emma knew how to barter, too. She was determined that the death of my mother would not isolate me from the other children in Sparta. She brought me to the playgrounds where white mothers gathered, and she slyly offered to mind the children "if you ladies have something else to do." They usually did, and eventually the children's playtime became circumscribed by the presence of "Aunt Emma and the little Yaffe boy."

Emma took remarks about my growth and weight personally, and wherever we went, there were the omnipresent thermos of milk and package of cookies. She didn't take kindly to references to the "little Yaffe boy." The mothers got the point, and soon we were regularly greeted with "My, how Bertram's growing!"

It was through music that Aunt Emma filled my immediate sense of absence from my mother. Fannie had a large, eclectic collection of records that she played on a Victrola, a mechanized portable phonograph that was always bedside during the final months of her illness. Now, wherever Emma's chores beckoned—kitchen, bath, or bedroom—we carried the Victrola, and she taught me to wind the machine and play the records. Rosa taught me to recognize, if not completely read, the labels, and Aunt Emma insisted that I announce the name and performer for each disk. While other children in Sparta were learning nursery rhymes and fables at the knees of their mothers, I became quite conversant with Enrico Caruso, Sigmund Romberg, Jerome Kern, Irving Berlin, Paul Whiteman, Joe "King" Oliver, and my favorite, Jelly Roll Morton.

Additionally there was the baby grand piano, which had an almost mystical significance in our home. It was my mother's last acquisition (just before Carl died), and she envisioned her children becoming proficient with the instrument. None of us had that particular aptitude, however, and Emma and I prevailed upon my father to let Emma's children and grandchildren practice hymns for their church choir. Sylvia, Emma's oldest daughter, had an ear for the piano. I would accompany her by beating on a toy drum. One day my father announced that we should stop the choir practice.

Emma protested. "Mr. Louis, Miss Fannie meant for that piano to be played."

My father thought about that and finally replied in that distinctive Yiddish drawl, "Maybe, Emma. But I don't think she'd appreciate her son going around singing 'Onward Christian Soldiers.'" We gradually played fewer hymns as Sylvia shaped my repertoire more toward Irving Berlin, George Gershwin, and tunes from her favorite group, the original Dixieland Jazz Band.

My father's resilience was enhanced by the determination that his and Fannie's children would be well-schooled, something that circumstance had denied him. Schooling and college always involved a negotiated compact: whatever one undertook must be completed. I did graduate from Emory University, but in 1941 while in my first year of law school I joined the navy's V-5 (officers' flight training) program. Then, with the advent of Pearl Harbor, I announced—not without trepidation—that I was switching to the Marine Corps and would not finish law school.

My father turned his head slightly and with that now-familiar gaze into the past—this time, no doubt, to Kovno Gibernya in Lithuania—he shrugged. "The damned Japanese are following us. They just won't let us finish our education."

In 1943 the Japanese caught up with me in the Solomon Islands in the South Pacific.

It was spellbinding, the blinding splendor of the vibrant purple, gold, green, black, and crimson rain forest of Bougainville that leaped before me at dawn on 3 November 1943. On the deck of an LST, I was preparing to bring the remaining units of Baker Company ashore to join the platoons that had landed on D day, 1 November. It was confounding: sea, blazing foliage, and sky suspended in a distracting encounter with naval gunfire, exploding artillery shells, and marine units preparing for assaults to enlarge the beachhead established by the landing teams.

Forcing myself to concentrate on the task at hand, I recovered from the daze that accompanied the vivid explosion of color. The mission of the 3d Marine Division, backed by the army's 37th Division, was to seize and protect an area on this Japanese-held island sufficient to accommodate two or three airfields which the Seabees would build as we expanded. Rapid deployment of reinforcements and supplies before the enemy could counterattack was critical. These airfields were necessary for the planned attack on the Japanese redoubt at Rabaul.

Once ashore, it was apparent that my initial impression was correct: nothing on this largest of the Solomon Islands was commonplace. In my experience, neither the astonishing Okefenokee Swamp south of the Georgia-Florida state line nor the jungles of Guadalcanal, where we trained and staged, compared to the overwhelming spectacle revealed directly and reflected in the waters of the magnificent bay.

Beneath the canopy of dense tropical forest was an abounding array of flora and fauna, all growing over a mat of mycorrhizal fungi specialized to absorb phosphorus and other chemical nutrients from the soil in a symbiotic relationship with the plants. My intense preoccupation with the concept of evolution paled before this immediate encounter with a teeming world of life, including the primitive natives, that had been sustained for eons. Fear of mortar and artillery barrages, fear of ambushes, and fear of nightly air raids commingled with the apprehension that nature would not tolerate the fiery intrusion without response.

The sun was fierce and the days humid, with temperatures often reaching a noontime high of one hundred degrees. This was usually followed by midafternoon rains that rapidly chilled the soaked terrain. Even relatively high areas became swampy breeding grounds for more insidious enemies: mosquitoes, spiders, and other insects whose bites could lead to malaria or ulceration and the dreaded "jungle rot." I was spared neither. Perpetual dampness and a lack of refrigeration posed the additional threats of trench foot and diarrhea.

I started out as executive officer of the company during the initial landing. About two weeks into the campaign, however, platoon leader Lt. Leon Stanley was killed as he tried to evacuate his tank when it was disabled by a land mine, so I took over his 2d Platoon. The role was not new to me, since I had trained as a platoon leader and was in charge of the training exercises for all the platoons in the company. When I assumed command, the platoon was attached to the 2d Battalion, 21st Marines, which was engaged in a final, yard-by-yard thrust to anchor the perimeter of the beachhead at the foot of a large hill mass known as Hellzapoppin Ridge. We were attempting to control the critical area at the junction of the Numa Numa and Piva trails. The tanks for that campaign were M3 Stuarts. Light tanks with four-man crews, the vehicles were small but relatively appropriate for the jungle terrain. We stayed in the tanks all night on the trail because we had to man the machine guns and the 37-mm weapons to protect the marines behind us and on our flanks.

I had never experienced claustrophobia during any of the training periods. Nor did it bother me during periods of combat when I was sufficiently focused on my objectives and conscious of the men about me. With the setting of the sun on my first day with the platoon, the little light that could penetrate the rich foliage and emerald tropical vegetation departed, and an impenetrable darkness set in. It was then that the protective armor surrounding me became a crypt. My breathing became labored, and my heart pounded with a ferocity I had never before experienced. This was not the normal fear or tension—even the anxiety—endemic to combat. I was drenched in a cold sweat from the claustrophobia and terrified by the thought that I might be experiencing a panic attack.

TWO *The Flux of Things*

That "all things flow" is the first vague generalization which the unsystematized, barely analyzed, intuition of men has produced. . . . and in all stages of civilization its recollection lends its pathos to poetry. . . . the flux of things is one ultimate generalization around which we must weave our philosophical system.

Alfred North Whitehead, *Process and Reality*

As perspiration chilled my body that first night on the trail in Bougainville, I realized that the encroaching panic was from claustrophobia and not from fear of combat. I divided the watches during the night into two-hour segments for each pair of us. Radio Operator Frank Rawcliffe and I shared a segment. Frank remained haunted by the futility of his repeated efforts to save Lieutenant Stanley, the platoon leader who—thinking that his tank, disabled by a mine, was ablaze—frantically tried to evacuate the vehicle and was immediately cut down by machine-gun fire. It remained a cautionary tale for all of us. On watch, my tension eased with my concentration on the external threat; the anxiety heightened, however, when I tried to rest or sleep. Striving to convince myself that my imagination was the immediate threat, I attempted, without much success, to transport my thoughts to other vistas—working out mathematical and chess problems and running through more idyllic terrain. I used these ploys while still keeping my faculties alert to the reality that we were surrounded by the enemy and that others depended on me. The effort was, of course, futile. Logic was no match for the irrational.

How could I exercise control over my body? In November 1943, at the age of twenty-three, I knew nothing about formal modes of meditation or imaging techniques as means of doing so. I had come to only a vague realization that contemplation was something worth trying to achieve, not to achieve any particular religious satisfaction but to respond to the philosophical imperative that was gnawing at me: if I was truly an instrument of evolution becoming aware of itself, then I must on occasion try to perceive things, with Spinoza, under the aspect of eternity.

I had already come to the conclusion that there could be no such thing as the definitive worldview. Reality was ongoing, its parts reciprocally affecting each other and thus changing reality with each encounter. All was flux and required continual redefinition. While still in New Zealand, before embarking for Guadalcanal, I had found a copy of Plutarch's *Moralia* and had come upon a vibrant passage that resonated with this view: "According to Heraclitus one cannot step twice into the same river, nor can one grasp any mortal substance in a stable condition, but by the intensity and rapidity of change it scatters and again gathers. Or rather not again nor later but at the same time it forms and dissolves, and approaches and departs."

I had also come across a copy of Heraclitus's *Fragments,* a compilation of pithy arguments and observations by a genius whose intuition has fired the imagination of philosophers, poets, and scientists throughout history. Fragment 124 I found compelling: "Graspings: Wholes and not wholes, convergent divergent, consonant dissonant, from all things one and from one thing all." It was grasping the oneness, the interconnectedness among things, that had been eluding me.

That night, at the junction of the Numa Numa and the Piva Trails, I struggled with these concepts. I began silently repeating the thought: "All things flow, and I am an integral, necessary part of all." It was a meaningless chant at first. After a while, the meaning began to penetrate. Although I had doubts, I noticed that my breathing was more normal, my pulse more regular. Even though I continued to be alert to my surroundings beyond the confines of the tank, I observed my situation with a detachment that served to carry me through this particular crisis.

It was 23 November 1943 and another miserable day on Bougainville. There was the elusive, ever-present enemy, the island's impenetrable walls of gnarled growth, and for marine tankers, other dispiriting frustrations. While the world's imagination was seized by the lightning exploits of German Panzer divisions, the wily, swift maneuvers of Rommel and Montgomery in the deserts of North Africa, and the massive tanks of Zhukov crushing the recoiling German armies across the plains from Stalingrad, the 3d Tank Battalion's mechanized chariots of combat were mired in the omnipresent mud of Bougainville. The main trails were mined and covered by artillery; when we veered from these, we either churned ourselves deeper and deeper into the muck or slid uncontrollably over inclines of clay. Our tools of choice were winches and steel cables to pull the armored vehicles back to some isolated bar of solid earth and try yet another route into action.

The next day—the day before Thanksgiving—the 9th and the main body of the 21st Regiments would strike straight ahead through the swamps to expand the beachhead. This would be remembered as the Battle of Piva Forks. My platoon was still attached to Lt. Col. Eustace Smoak's 2d Battalion, 21st Regiment, which had been advancing astride the Numa Numa Trail up to a point just short of the junction with East-West Road. Tomorrow the 2d Battalion would pivot south and protect the right flank of the drive.

Despite the limitations of our tanks' maneuverability, we had developed one tactic that Colonel Smoak found useful. Our 37-mm ammunition included an array of armor-piercing, high-explosive, and antipersonnel shells. The antipersonnels were canisters of "grapeshot" pellets that, in addition to being gruesomely effective against enemy soldiers, opened fields of fire through the thick foliage for Browning automatic rifles and light machine guns. While patrolling the Numa Numa Trail and setting up defensive positions each evening, the Stuart tanks became valued partners of the marine infantry.

For the morning of the twenty-fourth, Colonel Smoak wanted us in position off to the right of the Numa Numa Trail in an area called Coconut Grove. Although it was only about five hundred yards from our previous bivouac area, because of the rain it took the entire day to move into position and reconnoiter routes for the next morning so that we could move forward and protect the main attack.

At about 1600 we finally settled in the new bivouac area. Sgt. Richard Sprint and our five tank crews set about scraping mud from bodies, weapons, and vehicles and digging foxholes. I took Cpl. Eddie Luscavage and reported to Colonel Smoak. The colonel marked our position on his map and informed me that we would be assigned to his E Company tomorrow.

He asked very pointedly, "Can you move those tanks forward without getting back on the trail?"

"We did today, Colonel. There are some off-trail routes that the engineers cleared for the AMTRACs [amphibian tractors]. Of course, it's been raining all day. We'll check it out at dawn again."

Colonel Smoak gave his usual laconic response. "We'll see. I'll contact you sometime after 0600. Be ready."

"Yes, sir." Nobody saluted on Bougainville. None of the officers particularly wanted to be saluted, what with snipers hanging from trees everywhere.

Luscavage, a tank driver, was dubious as we started back toward our area. "Lieutenant, I hope for your sake those tanks can churn out of this crap. That colonel can be tough."

I returned to our tanks and joined Radio Operator Rawcliffe; our gunner, Bill Prillaman; and my driver, John Martel. As we opened K rations and scrounged for dry socks and underwear we had squirreled away in the Stuarts, Dick Sprint and the other tank commanders joined us.

"What's the word for tomorrow, Lieutenant?" Sprint asked.

"We'll be with Easy Company again. They want us up there, but not on the trail. They want to keep that clear for the AMTRACs carrying casualties to the hospital. We'll move as far forward as we can on the routes we tried today. We'll test it out at dawn."

Sprint shook his head. "I don't know. There's been a lot of rain."

I looked over at Bill Prillaman. His helmet, suspended on a string of communication wire between two bayonets, was being heated by flames from canned heat. "What the hell are you doing, Prillaman?"

Prillaman's blue eyes danced as he drawled, "Well, I went over there." He pointed to a 21st Marine chow line. "They gave me some cubes of bouillon soup and tomato juice." He looked to Rawcliffe. "You know those cans of meat and beans I've been saving? Well, Lieutenant, this is Bougainville mulligan stew. I've got enough for you, too, Lieutenant. I even dipped my helmet in the three barrels of water. It's *clean* Bougainville mulligan stew."

I didn't hesitate. "I think I'll take you up on that offer." I handed over my mess gear. I can't remember many meals that I enjoyed more. Everyone tasted it.

Soon a member from each tank crew, helmet in hand, drifted over to the infantry chow line with parting instructions for Prillaman: "Keep that fire hot, Bill."

It was getting dark when Dick Sprint looked at me with a knowing smile. "Tell me something, Lieutenant." I recognized I was in for some sardonic observation. He continued, "What did they teach at Fort Knox that could be helpful out here?"

I thought about his question. It was the U.S. Army's cavalry divisions that supplied the techniques, tactics, and officers to form America's armored corps at the beginning of World War II. It was a natural transition from one mode of mobile warfare to another. Cavalry personnel, culled from the plains of Kansas and Texas, joined at Fort Knox, which became the training and staging ground for General Patton's armored divisions in 1941.

The Marine Corps had no cavalry tradition to draw upon. From scratch, the 1st Tank Battalion was formed at New River, North Carolina, the 2d Tank Battalion at Camp Elliott in San Diego. In 1942, as General Patton's legions were leaving for North Africa, I was among a cadre of marine officers assigned to Fort Knox for tank tactics training. The tactical instructors were well-indoctrinated in Patton's vision of rapid, daring attacks over incredible distances and unlikely terrain. Fuel levels were at least as important as ammo supplies.

I went along with Sprint's wry mood. "I learned a lot, Dick." I nodded toward my tank. "That baby can travel forty-five, fifty miles an hour. If the Seabees and engineers would just pave these damned roads, we could go from one end of Bougainville to the other in less than two hours. Shooting machine guns, firing 37-mm cannons, waving .45s, and flinging grenades everywhere, we'd frighten the hell out of the bastards. Problem is, the Seabees and engineers are just building airstrips and draining swamps."

Luscavage laughed. "Fifty miles an hour? We didn't move fifty yards in three days until this morning. We haven't gone over twenty miles an hour since we left New Zealand."

I shrugged, and we all smiled in recognition of the truth of Eddie's observation. After a while I announced, "It'll be dark soon. If anybody's sleeping in the tanks, stay there. Don't go moving around. The marines over there are expecting infiltration tonight. The Japs know very well what we are planning tomorrow. Those marines'll be firing at any noise over here."

I looked at the foxhole Rawcliffe and I would be sharing. Although the rain had stopped, the pit was already filled with three or four inches of seeping water. I got up and spread my poncho over the wet mud. The night of 23 November, with oozing mud, mosquitoes, scorpions, and three red-alert air raids was a typical night on Bougainville.

On the morning of the twenty-fourth, fifteen minutes before the beginning of the drive (H minus 15), the artillery battalions of the 12th Marines and the 37th Infantry Division poured tons of steel, the heaviest concentration yet, on the Japanese positions. Although we knew it was going to happen, it was astonishing and unsettling as thirty-six hundred rounds of 75-mm and 105-mm high explosives whistled overhead and blasted an eight-hundred-square-yard area less than twenty-five hundred yards in front of us. Above those missiles were the whooshing 155-mms, heading for more distant hills. As the marines moved out, the whirring 81-mm and 60-mm mortars exploded on more immediate targets just ahead. Finally, with the rat-a-tat of the machine guns, the push was on!

Before and during this deafening barrage, Sergeant Sprint and I jockeyed the tanks forward to be in a defensive position just behind the lines of departure in case of counterattack. My tank, Sprint's, and one other were on the makeshift trail parallel to Numa Numa when the fourth Stuart failed to get any traction in the churning muck. I took off my dungaree top and left it with my .45 side arm and belt in the tank to protect them from the flying mud as we labored to secure the cable and hoist the flailing iron whale forward. I put on my steel helmet but did not secure it because I expected to be back in my tank shortly.

The noise level from the shelling and racing of engines made normal conversation impossible. Corporal Luscavage grabbed my arm and pointed to a runner from Colonel Smoak. The colonel and Captain Altman from E Company wanted me at the command post immediately. I told Luscavage to follow me as I motioned to Sprint to carry on with the chore of pulling the last two tanks into formation.

As I approached the 2d Battalion command post, a bunker of logs and sandbags, I was confidently preparing to report that I would have four, maybe five, tanks in any position Captain Altman would designate. I noticed Colonel Smoak was scowling and pointing to me. When I was within shouting distance, I learned why.

"You goddamned idiot!" he growled. "Secure that fucking helmet! And if I ever see you without your goddamned weapon again, I'll kick my foot so far up your ass, they'll have to take both of us to the hospital to get it out!"

I secured my helmet, but at that moment all hell broke loose among the American marines and soldiers on the Empress Augusta Bay beachhead. The Japanese unleashed a coordinated barrage of artillery fire, moving up and down our positions with uncanny accuracy.

"Christ almighty!"

"Hit the deck! Hit the deck!!"

There were screeching, ripping sounds—like tearing of huge can-vas sheets—mingled with flashes of fire as the high-explosive shells burst upon contact with the tall trees. A hailstorm of searing steel fragments fell everywhere among us. Fragments everywhere.

"Medic! For God's sake! Corpsman!"

There were no unoccupied foxholes in the area for Luscavage and me. We dove to the ground next to the bunker, desperately trying to melt into the footing of the structure. The rounds that didn't burst above exploded with frightful ferocity on the jungle floor, sending ricocheting metal in all directions. One shell fell amid a squad of infantrymen between us and the trail. I saw an arm fly from the hole of mud, blood, and mangled flesh. Burning fragments of iron sailed into the sand and wood above my head.

"Corpsman! Medic! For God's sake!"

The barrage lasted for only about five minutes, but this artillery attack and two more that occurred in the morning inflicted the heaviest marine casualties of the Bougainville campaign.

After the shelling had stopped, no one seemed sure when to get up. Finally Captain Altman came over and murmured, "Come on. I know where we have to go. Let's get up there." As we silently walked to the trail past the disfigured bodies of exposed muscle and slivers of bone, I was thankful for being alive—and not having to continue the confrontation with Colonel Smoak.

This day, 24 November, despite determined resistance and sev-eral counterattacks, marines advanced another twelve hundred yards—which was a lot. Today would also be remembered by the 3d Marine Division for something else.

The remarkable Seabees and engineers had finished the Torokina air landing strip, and while the Battle of Piva Forks was raging, planes brought in fresh provisions including turkey, rolls, and what was purported to be cranberry sauce. Roasted over open fires, boiled in GI cans, and warmed in any other conceivable manner, the meals were distributed throughout the division, including frontline battle positions. During the raging Battle of Piva Forks, we celebrated Thanksgiving on Bougainville. Personally, I didn't enjoy the meal. The turkey was greasy, my heart was still racing, my stomach still churning from the artillery storm, and I could not rid myself of the image of Lieutenant Colonel Smoak and me at the field hospital for his foot extraction.

The Battle of Piva Forks secured the beachhead for the marines, and the Seabees finished the bomber strip—the second and larger airfield. The marine aircraft wing was now in position to pulverize and neutralize Rabaul, the feared Japanese bastion that had controlled the South Pacific. Colonel Smoak's 2d Battalion—with my 2d Platoon, Company B, tanks still attached—moved forward to secure and protect the critical area surrounding Hill 600 on the southern perimeter of the beachhead. On many nights, however, the Japanese made forays into our positions. It was in repelling these attacks with grapeshot that Sergeant Sprint and I agreed: we had devised a tank tactic to teach at Fort Knox.

A few days after the fierce artillery exchange on Thanksgiving Day, there were rumors that our aircraft spotted eruptions from the volcanic hills beyond the beachhead perimeter. Indeed, on 10 December a series of tremors began. The quakes continued throughout the island for several days. The sudden appearance of fissures in the ground and the spontaneous uprooting of trees produced in us feelings of disequilibrium and frightening uncertainty. It now seems far-fetched, but at the time I did wonder if there wasn't some substance to my original apprehension that nature would not tolerate these fiery intrusions without responding.

THREE *The Stillness*

In the last analysis it is the ultimate picture which an age forms of the nature of its world that is its most fundamental possession. It is the final controlling factor in all thinking whatever.

Edwin A. Burtt, *The Metaphysical Foundations of Modern Physical Science*

The exchange of letters between Erna and me took an ironic turn during the weeks I was aboard the *Gunston Hall*. She always infused the most mundane events with an excitement that made me smile. She wrote a V-mail (an airmail letter written on a special form) almost every day and more lengthy letters once, sometimes twice, weekly. The accumulated correspondence on each of the two mail calls was the highlight of that period for me. Her letters were so full of spontaneity and liveliness that I instinctively reached for her hand while reading.

Although I was preparing for combat, the repetitive routine left me with few things to write her about. Each day was identical to the one before. More and more I elaborated on details about marines whom she knew personally or was acquainted with from my character sketches. I gave a progress report on Master Sergeant Riley's daughter, Patty, who was born four months after we left the States. Erna had met Riley when we were loading at San Diego. He was obsessive in exhibiting Patty's photographs month after month. "Warrant Officer Newton posted the latest picture on the bulletin board so we wouldn't be pestered individually. Jim Riley was not happy but got over it when we all celebrated Patty's first birthday a couple of weeks ago," I wrote.

And there was Thornhill. Erna knew how intrigued I was with Corporal Thornhill. Although records claimed he was eighteen, we all knew he was no more than sixteen, having lied about his age when enlisting two years earlier. With brown curly hair and sparkling eyes to match, Thornhill personified vitality and life even in the midst of his frequent and annoying adolescent mischief. "He has little education, and when I censor his mail, I have to restrain myself from editing, however gently, the letters to his sister. He lists her as next-of-kin, and I suspect he is an orphan. Beyond his forced bravado he has an exuberance that reminds me of you. And then occasionally I glimpse him standing apart looking out to sea, and I think of my father coming to America alone at about that age. Strange that someone reminds me both of you and my father. Thornhill's fine."

Then there was the ship's doctor. How could I write about him without revealing that we were in transit to combat? "The navy has sent the battalion another doctor. 'Doc' is a real character, far older than most of us—he must be nearing fifty. Loves talking deep and considers himself an authority on William James's philosophy. But then I understand most Harvard graduates do. He's a great chess player. We have an ongoing bet: if I win a game, he will certify me as fit only for stateside duty. Don't expect me home tomorrow. He's really good."

I kept her apprised of Tom Murphy, who was on sentry duty when I first reported to Company B at Camp Lejeune. She identified the company with Murph. "Just left Tom a little while ago. He always asks for the 'missus.' I never asked you, but how do you like being a 'missus'?"

As I approached a group of my men, there was no mistaking that the second mail call aboard the *Gunston Hall* had improved our moods. It was my usual visit about dusk. I veered toward a circle of tank crewmen gathered around the "old salts," Gunnery Sgts. Charles Buckner and Milton Dabbert—"China hands" who were probably spinning tales about "the old corps."

"How's the missus, Skipper?" Sergeant Murphy queried.

"She's fine, Murph. Always asks for you."

"Beautiful lady," Murph mused.

I turned to Buckner. "Don't let me interrupt, Buck. Where are we tonight? Shanghai?" I teased.

"Naw, I'm telling these young biddies what it was like to be aboard ship in days while they were still pecking corn around their mother hens."

"I could go for some corn now," interjected Sgt. Bruce Bronson.

"Yeah. Corn whiskey," said Sergeant Dabbert. This brought

laughter. Bronson was well-known for his capacity in drinking the hard stuff.

Lt. Charlie Kirkham, a former enlisted man, had joined us. He pointed to Buckner and Dabbert. "I don't think these guys ever remember *not* being in the corps."

"Maybe not," Dabbert replied, "but we saw this war coming a long time ago. We shoulda been ready."

Sergeant Sprint looked over at me. "Cap'n, Lieutenant Stanley told me you quit law school to join the corps in 1940. Why would you do that?"

"That wasn't quite the way it was. I didn't actually quit school. I did apply for the naval air corps V-5 program while I was in college in 1940. But I had a deviated septum, and they didn't accept me until early in 1941 when they changed the qualifications. The acceptance came through while I was finishing my first year of law school. But the navy had it right the first time. It was hard for me to breathe flying in open cockpits. I had an operation after a couple of months at Anacostia, but it didn't help. The navy offered to accept me in the V-7 program for officers. I had reason to believe war was coming, and I wanted to be well-trained. The marines stationed at Anacostia convinced me that this was the place to be." I laughed and pointed at Buchner and Dabbert. "Besides, where else in the service could I find old salts like those guys to teach me how to survive?"

Sprint persisted. "How did you know the war was coming?"

I paused, wondering how to explain what my illiterate father had taught me while I thought I was teaching him.

At the age of fourteen, Louis Yaffe brought more to the States than the ten dollars sewn in the lining of his coat and the identification card strung around his neck. From his family in the shtetl he carried a legacy of insatiable curiosity about the world as well as an inherent wariness nurtured by legends and by the reality of sudden, violent forays by Cossacks, the arch anti-Semitic Muscovites. From his rare reminiscences I pieced together a picture of impassioned family forums conducted at mealtime, probably instigated by the two older "radical" brothers, devoted to arguments against czarist oppression and visions of a different, better world. For the transplanted Louis, these memories were recast into an obsessive love for America with the freedom it afforded him and what I perceived to be paranoia about any semblance of anti-Semitism.

In my early teens I became adept at scanning and reading to my father articles from the Atlanta *Journal.* He also subscribed to the *Day,* a Yiddish newspaper published in New York, as supplemental nourishment for his appetite for current events. Nearing the age of fifteen, I became impatient with the practice of digesting the news for my father; he would question me about events that he insinuated I was not divulging, and it annoyed me. Our ongoing dialogue about news coverage had both immediate and long-range effects.

At Sparta High School I became not only the resident authority on what I jokingly called the news-of-the-*Day* but also the editor of our weekly column for the local paper. Journalism, I decided, would be my major in college.

Something else was happening that I appreciated only in retrospect. The tenuous connection that my father maintained with his sister in West Virginia—who, like my mother, was named Fannie—was through envelopes that I would address and into which he would insert cash. Some weeks after each mailing, he would get a letter from Fannie that included brief notes from my grandparents in Kovno Gubernya, acknowledging the money and not saying much else other than that "things were bad." During 1934 and 1935 my father was insistent that I look for news about Lithuania. While there was ample news about Hitler's and Mussolini's aggression against their neighboring states, there was precious little written about what my father called the "persecution of the people."

"Nothing about Lithuania?"

"No."

"Poland?"

"Nope."

"Rumania?"

"Nothing."

He shook his head and, tracing his finger along the newsprint, moved his lips haltingly as he returned to the *Day*. It was in late 1935 that Aunt Fannie called and said she was worried. She had not received any answers to the last two letters.

In 1936 I came across an item quoting a European news source in the *Journal* about the Nuremberg laws in Germany that specifically applied to Jews. "Did you know about this?" I asked.

He nodded. "That happened last year."

"See, there *is* some news about what is happening," I remarked.

"Very *some*." It came in his best Southern Yiddish accent. "It's not just about the Jews. But that's Germany. They won't understand."

Nor did I. In Sparta, I had no impression of being different except that I was presumed to know more about the Old Testament than my friends—which I didn't. My father did not necessarily want to disabuse me of that perception, but time after time, question by question, he did educate me about things that I only began to piece together while seriously studying the press in my first years at Emory.

The Jews in Germany and Western Europe were slow to recognize or believe what was happening, even after the Nuremberg laws of 1935 deprived them of citizenship. Eastern Europe, on the other hand, had a long-standing tradition of more overt anti-Semitism. Hitler's rise to power was quickly hailed by Eastern Europeans, and the Jews of Lithuania, Poland, and Latvia felt the effects immediately; they understood what was happening. Without explicitly lecturing me, my father was teaching me the significance of an insight I was gleaning from some of the authors I was reading, John Dos Passos and Ernest Hemingway among them: ask not for whom the bell tolls.

I gave Sergeant Sprint a shorter answer. "Actually I made up my mind to enter the service long before I went to law school. I was studying to be a professional journalist, and I thought that a year of law while I was waiting to be accepted for officer's training would round out my education."

"A journalist?" It came from Corporal Thornhill, who had been unusually intent on the conversation.

"One who studies writing and interpreting the news." I laughed at the irony. "My father, an immigrant from Eastern Europe, taught me how to *really* read the news." I looked appreciatively over at Dabbert. "Like Sergeant Dabbert, I saw the war coming early on."

I continued my letter to Erna, "Murph sends his best—he's really fond of you."

And there was Quentin Joy. "Joy is working out well. I made a good choice in selecting him to be executive officer of the company. He sends his regards and enjoys most of the books and magazines you send me but suggests he can do with a little less philosophy. That is a funny observation coming from him, since last night we spent two hours talking about the nature of reality."

We had been talking about the metarational. What had led me to raise that issue with Joy was the difference between the two philosophies represented by Bertrand Russell and Henri Bergson.

For me, as for many of my contemporaries, Bertrand Russell was a revered mentor in matters moral and philosophical. His attempt to forge a truly scientific philosophy was most compatible with minds dubious of political, religious, and moral dogma. According to Russell, reason was the arbiter between mirage and reality. My admiration for Russell notwithstanding, I was intrigued with Henri Bergson's advocacy of "intuition as the faculty whereby we penetrate to the truth of things and feel the inner pulse of reality."

One's view of reality is a unique, fundamental possession, and as Edwin Burtt said, "the final controlling factor in all thinking whatever." It seemed to me that reality is ultimately an instinctive construct and to that extent is, despite our protests, intuitive.

This dissonance between the two philosophies—intellect versus intuition—had lain fallow in my mind for some time. While reading Julian Huxley, the eminent British biologist, I determined to resolve my ambivalent attitude toward intuition. "It is perfectly possible," Huxley wrote, "that today man's [intuitive] faculties are in the same case as were his mathematical faculties during the first or second glaciations of the Ice Age—barely more than a potentiality, with no technique for eliciting and developing them, no tradition behind them to give them continuity and intellectual respectability." This thought convinced me that, with sufficient effort on one's part, these two forms of conscious activity could attain their full development.

Contemplating distinctions among the categories of thought—rational, irrational, and metarational—led me through this philosophical impasse. The metarational insists on using the intellectual faculties to the utmost, then proceeds beyond that point to the intuitive.

I thought I would pass this by Joy and Doc.

"What the hell is that?" Joy scowled.

"The metarational?" Doc's eyebrows arched far above the rim of his glasses, almost melding with his head of thick graying hair. "There's no such thing. No word, *metarational.*"

"I know," I said. "That's what intrigues me. There should be. Metarationality is a completion rather than a rejection of reason and science."

"William James called these spiritual excitements 'over-beliefs,'" Doc reminded us. "He wasn't apologetic about them.

He felt the most interesting and valuable things about a man are usually his over-beliefs. They are absolutely indispensable. We should treat them with tenderness and tolerance as long as they are not intolerant themselves."

"Ah, I like that!" Joy said—an unusually swift judgment for him. Joy usually deliberated longer before responding. We were in the officers' mess, and when he rose and walked over to the burner for a cup of coffee, it occurred to me that his six-foot frame always seemed much larger indoors.

I demurred. "Tenderness and tolerance are not the point. Intuition, after the full exercise of reason, is something different than intuition without, against, or instead of reason. It's more than a gut feeling, although it may be that too. Just as the rational is the perception of the logical implication of what is, the metarational is the not-illogical intuition of what may be. It's *honest* intuition."

"Honest intuition?" Doc shook his head. "Captain, if you're aiming to coin a phrase, you fall far short of Oscar Wilde or George Bernard Shaw."

Joy agreed. "It's more like *Alice in Wonderland*. It means what you say it means. Besides, it's a fuckin' contradiction. . . . It's an oxy . . . oxy. . . ."

"Oxymoron," Doc said. "Bert, in your search for reality, what's your problem with science? Our capacity for reason has provided freedom from drudgery, improved health, enhanced quality of lives, and given us incredible modes of communication and transportation. Rational inquiry also gives us a description of reality, however incomplete and forever changing—always, as you're fond of saying, 'in process.'"

"That's the point, Doc," I insisted. "Description, not *understanding*. Our capacity for reason, however necessary, is insufficient to lead us to comprehending the ongoing, creative cosmic process. Whatever you call that process—nature, evolution, God—it experiences the world only through our consciousness.

Can intellect grasp the one thing from which all things flow? Or are our finite minds too rooted in time and space? Science, at its best, never pretends to reveal the meaning of life; it offers veto power over superstition and metaphysical error. Meaning is something else."

Doc shook his head and looked at Quentin Joy. "God only experiences the world through you. What do you think, Lieutenant?"

There was the characteristic delay as Joy rose to return the coffee mug. "What do *I* think?" He returned and sat across from me. "I think my skipper has either been on the deck by himself far too long or"—he looked at me and half smiled—"not quite long enough."

I shrugged, looked at the time, and reached for the chess set. "I have time for one game before the changing of the watch. Who's the victim?"

Doc started lining up the pieces. "You are."

My arguments to Joy and the Doc may not have been compelling, but during those nights on the deck of the *Gunston Hall* I came to terms with the metarational—it was *honest* intuition.

I woke with a start. The silence was stifling. There was not a ripple as far as the eye could see; the ocean was a sheet of glass. I had never experienced anything quite as astonishing as the immense stillness of the Pacific becalmed. Nothing was familiar. It was just before dawn, and crewmen and marines on the *Gunston Hall* seemed to ooze from their quarters and inexplicably spoke in whispers. Suddenly the sun, unclouded, vaulted upward and revealed an unwalled vastness, breathtakingly still. The calm, which lasted until early afternoon, added considerably to our sense of confinement and impatience. Things changed that evening—we received orders for W day. The Guam landing would be 0830, Friday, 21 July—thirteen days away.

The pounding began.

Guam is the largest and most populous of the Mariana Islands. Peanut-shaped, it is thirty-two miles long and four to eight and a half miles wide. There had been sporadic B-24 bombing and battleship shelling during the month-long delay. Beginning on 8 July, however, and day and night thereafter as the armada converged on the island, the pounding was unceasing. Navy and Marine Corps fighter-bomber groups and rocket launchers joined the cacophony as W day approached.

There were twenty thousand Japanese soldiers on Guam who, after the devastating sea battles of June, knew that they would not receive support and that there was no place for strategic retreat. Off shore, there were nearly fifty-five thousand marines and GIs who were well-trained and indoctrinated in the basic assault tactical concept of "sooner better than later, get it the hell over with."

The evening bombings and cruiser-battleship shelling masked the forays of navy frogmen, who were blowing up tank traps and many of the mines on the coral beaches as well as reconnoitering for protruding reefs—explorations for which the tank crews were particularly grateful. Still, the din of the unrelenting bombardment wore thin on our nerves. At breakfast, 0400 Friday morning, 21 July, after fifty-four days aboard ship, clearly we were ready.

Despite the size of the island, the rugged volcanic hills, coral cliffs, and dense jungle gave few if any options for an assault landing led by tanks. The 3d Marine Division would land from the west on a twenty-five-hundred-yard front in the crescent of Apra Harbor between Adelup and Asan Points. There were some coral reefs, but they were negotiable. If the Japanese had had any doubts about our landing area, the severe preinvasion bombings on the beach strip dispelled them. There would be no feigned maneuvers in this battle. The 3d Marine Regiment would take the left flank, the 21st Regiment the center, and the 9th Marines the southern right flank. The 1st Provisional Brigade would simultaneously land five miles farther south.

Our Company B tanks would be a support unit for the 21st Regiment. Our objectives: to neutralize the area between the beaches and the cliffs directly ahead as the marines landed, to coordinate with the infantry in a ground assault along the tropical jungle defiles through which flowed the branches of the Asan River, and, finally, to seize the high ground of Fonte Ridge, which began about a thousand yards inland.

Company B now had replaced its eighteen light tanks with the more effective medium Sherman tanks with five-man crews. Of our fifteen Shermans, the headquarters tanks and the 1st and 2d Platoons would be in the first wave and were with me on the *Gunston Hall.* Lieutenant Kirkham, his 3d Platoon, and a tank recovery unit would follow in the next wave. There were four tanks to each of the three platoons and one tank each for me and the company executive officer, Quentin Joy. A third headquarters tank was equipped with a bulldozer and was commanded by Gunnery Sergeant Sprint. Each vehicle had a 75-mm gun, a .30-caliber machine gun in the bow, and another that could be used when the turret hatch was open. Three of the tanks had flamethrowers to be used against caves. Each tank company had a formidable array of weapons.

I spent my last few nights on the deck of the *Gunston Hall* rememorizing the terrain of the landing area on the maps that we were given with the explicit warning that they were pre-1941 and perhaps unreliable. Nevertheless, I memorized the number of feet of every elevation and depression and the number of yards between the branches of the Asan at various points inland. Mostly, I visualized each tank crew and the desired position we would maintain as we hit the beach. There was concern about communication between tanks and the infantry. In addition to the hand-held signal corps radio sets for the liaison men, we had installed phones on the "grouser boxes" on the outside of the tanks. I wasn't sure how this would work in combat. And always, there was the specter of Chonito Cliffs on our left, which was the objective of the 3d Marines.

There was also another specter to be reckoned with. During the assaults on Tarawa in the Gilbert Islands, the reefs and unseasonably low tides prevented the landing craft from bringing the troops and the tanks up to the beaches. In certain instances the LCMs were either ripped by protruding coral or the ramps were lowered too soon and the craft loaded with tanks, all hatches buttoned up, sank in twenty to forty feet of water, drowning the crews.

My concentration was intense. It relaxed only when I thought of Erna and tried to devise a way to phrase and deceptively date my letters so that she would not be aware of my exact frame of mind or my whereabouts during these days. Later I discovered that I had not been successful. My observation about Thornhill looking out to sea revealed more than I had intended.

We were now close enough that the thundering and pounding were accompanied by flashes of fire, especially vivid at night. There seemed never a moment without the booming peals of shelling and bombing. I wondered how the human beings on Guam could possibly endure this.

At 0530 on W day, the officers and tank commanders assembled on the deck immediately above the dock that encased the tanks. The aft gate had been raised, and we were taking on water slowly to buoy the LCMs. I found it sobering that the men were so attentive as I went through a plan that had become a boring litany for weeks, months.

The point of departure would be an imaginary line fifteen hundred yards offshore. The navy crewmen would line the LCMs abreast using my tank as guide—Lieutenant Cavender and the 2d Platoon on my left with Executive Officer Joy to my immediate left and Lieutenant Warden with the 1st Platoon on my immediate right. "Try to keep this order as we hit the beach," I instructed them. "Shoot at any moving object directly ahead. If you strike a mine or are hit with mortars, stay in your tank." Lieutenant Stanley was still very much in my mind. "We will protect you; the retriever tank and the 3d Platoon will be right behind us. Company C tanks and the 3d Marine Regiment are on our left, charging Adelup Point and those damned cliffs. Company A tanks are on our right but will turn south to take Asan Point. Concentrate on the ground and hills directly ahead of us. Go in as far as you can until I give the order to stop. When the marines reach us, I will get orders on how to proceed with them. Have your drivers turn over the engines once between now and 0630. At 0700 I'll be in my tank, and we'll have one radio check, then keep radio silence."

With the Tarawa debacle in mind, I was not surprised that most of their shoes were untied. "You can keep the hatches open until you get to the line of departure." Again with Tarawa in mind, I knew most of them would probably throw open the hatches soon after we left the line. "The skipper of this ship will signal the LCMs when to leave the line about 0815. I will pump my arm twice to signal the close of the hatches."

The shelling was increasing in intensity—a crescendo ever deepening, never-ending. There was genuine eye contact when I asked for the final time, "Any questions?" I waited until I received an answer from each of the officers and men.

"All set, Cap'n."

"We're ready."

"All set, Skipper."

"No questions."

At 0800 I was standing in the turret awed by the precision with which the LCMs fell into formation at the line of departure. To our left Company C was in place, and far to my right the boats carrying Company A were lining up. Behind us, as far as I could see, there were ranks of landing craft—Higgins boats and amphibian tractors—filled with marines waiting to take our place as we left the line of departure. Behind them were the larger—by comparison, almost behemoth—LSTs with artillery and Seabee equipment and personnel. With the exception of navy frogmen who had been exploring the beaches for several nights, the marines in the tanks would be among the first to hit the shore. It was an immense array of craft, tanks, sailors, and marines. I was surprised at how relaxed I was, observing the whole process. Everything was going exactly as we planned and as I had imagined. I remember being especially pleased at the confidence I had in my men and that I felt they had in me. I was eager to get on with it.

I was not thinking of anything beyond Company B, 3d Tank Battalion, 3d Marine Division, and a sector of the beachhead to the immediate front. My mind became even more focused as I reflected that for the immediate future—minutes and hours—my life was inextricably intertwined with the lives of the four marines in my tank—Elmer Kanocz, the driver; Tom Murphy, the assistant driver and machine gunner; Ed Luscavage, the gunner; and Everett Shrock, the radioman and loader—and two navy men: a young Chinese seaman, Yee, who would lower the ramp of the LCM when we reached the beach, and the coxswain, who for some reason was called Blackie. At this point, it was Blackie who really controlled our destiny. Each time I caught his eye, I received a thumbs-up signal, reinforcing a commitment he had been making all morning: "Don't worry. I'll put you on that beach. I promise!" Going into combat, I felt particularly fortunate being with these four marines and the two seamen.

It was a clear, arid day. The dryness was a relief to me. I noticed that the fungus was drying and my skin was rapidly healing. Through binoculars I scrutinized the island ahead. It seemed less than fifteen hundred yards away. Those dark spots at the foot of the hills and cliffs could be caves, antitank guns. I wondered if Joy had picked up the briefing map in the mess hall. He was standing in his tank on a rocking LCM about fifty feet to my left, his eyes riveted on me. I must have smiled as I turned toward him, guessing his thought: "We don't need the fuckin' map, Bert. We're there!" Later he asked me what I had found so amusing at the line.

Suddenly the stillness poured forth. Sometime before 0815 the guns fell silent, and the rocket-laden dive-bombers and strafing planes departed. We knew this would happen when the smaller gunboats prepared to take over and protect us as we charged the beaches. I am sure there were rumblings of motors, engines, perhaps planes strafing the far hills, but after the past two weeks this was silence—a profound, disconcerting absence of the familiar.

In this stillness, a thought came over me: the cosmos was searching for self-awareness through me, billions of me's. This ascent into quiet contemplation—not as an observer, not for any intellectual satisfaction, not as a busy religious ritual, not for surcease from a gnawing hunger for immortality, not in other-worldly isolation from the pain and poignancy of the world of things but as a passionate participant in the ultimate reality that defies description—was the meaning of life. Yet it wasn't me but universal life that was seeking meaning. For an instant, as this intuition filtered through to me, and despite the disharmony between contemplation and impending action, I felt at one with the cosmos. At the same time I understood that mine was a fleeting insight, one that had arrived only when I had abandoned all effort to lay hold of it.

There were simultaneous signal flashes from the decks of all the ships behind us. The engines of the landing craft revved up, and as we departed the line, I pumped my right arm twice, and all the hatches closed.

FOUR *Fragmentation*

For heroic achievement in connection with operations against the enemy while serving as commanding officer of a Marine tank company on Guam, Mariana Islands, from 21 July to 11 August 1944. Captain Yaffe personally acted as advisor to infantry commanders, and directed the formation and employment of tank-infantry teams in the reduction of enemy defenses. On the night of 26 July 1944 he was painfully wounded by a Japanese grenade but continued to carry on. His professional ability, initiative, and appreciation of the problems of infantry-tank operations and his resourcefulness in maintaining his company continuously at a high standard of combat efficiency contributed materially to the success of the operation. His untiring efforts were in keeping with the highest traditions of the United States Naval Service.

**Maj. Gen. G. B. Erskine, USMC, awarding the
Bronze Star to Captain Yaffe, 8 July 1945**

It was the night of 25 July, the morning of the twenty-sixth, and courage was plentiful. The W day landings on Guam became a model for amphibious assaults. The navy, the marines, and the 77th Infantry Division of the army were driven by the determination to recapture American territory and carry the battle to the enemy. Blackie and his mates placed us firmly on the beaches. We had worked out an innovative technique for avoiding the landing craft problems of the Tarawa debacle. If the LCM struck coral, prior to lowering the ramp we eased the tank forward. This tested whether the LCM was grounded safely. If the craft were not grounded, the bow sank; but the ramp being up, the tank could be backed into position again and a new landing place found.

The shock that the Japanese suffered from the preinvasion shelling allowed our tanks enough time to cross the reefs and provide protective fire for the marines who were immediately following. Despite the horrendous shelling, however, it soon became apparent that the enemy had ample artillery and mortars available. They also had the high ground surrounding the beachhead.

At first, the mortar and artillery shells seemed to fall at random, and the beach casualties were light. Our 75-mms and machine guns responded quickly to any activity and we managed to silence a three-inch gun emplacement on the slope of Fonte Ridge, immediately ahead of us. Within minutes we reached our intermediate objective near the mouth of the Asan River. With Sergeant Murphy covering me, we left our tank and, as planned, contacted the reconnaissance team of the 3d Battalion, 21st Marines, who directed us to the regimental headquarters digging in to our right. As I was receiving orders from the commanding officer, Colonel Butler, Japanese mortars pummeled the reconnaissance party we had just left. Almost all of them were killed.

My orders were to support the infantry as far as we could go into the ravines, reconnoiter for possible tank routes up the slopes between Chonito Cliffs on our left and Fonte Ridge, and protect the shore parties as they established field hospitals and supply depots. A key factor in any assault is the rapidity with which supplies, heavy equipment, support artillery, and reserve personnel reach shore. These reinforcements kept coming.

Lieutenant Kirkham and our 3d Platoon arrived, and I sent him with Lieutenant Joy to establish a command post with the company communications jeep near Colonel Butler's post and to be available for a defense of the beach. Lieutenant Warden's 1st Platoon and two of the 2d Platoon's tanks were to advance as far as possible with the 21st Marines. Sergeant Sprint and I— with Lieutenant Cavender, two of his tanks, and a squad of infantry—reconnoitered routes up the ridge.

The enemy returned fire from well-camouflaged caves, concrete shelters, and wooded areas along the ravines. Their mortars and artillery were becoming more focused and were coordinated with counterassaults by soldiers. These attacks by relatively small squads were ferocious. The enemy showed a pointless disregard for their own lives as they charged the marines, and even the tanks, with small arms and grenades. Always grenades. The battle was an alternating rhythm of marines and tanks attacking caves and wooded ravines followed by savage counterassaults from Japanese descending the ridges below the Fonte–Mount Tenjo Road, the key objective for us. It was a bizarre scene: cows, goats, and chickens wandered in a drunken daze among the marines and Japanese. Our casualties were heavy, and navy medical corpsmen began to run out of stretchers. Names of some of the wounded were painfully familiar: Private First Class Schaeffer, Sergeant Edgecomb. . . .

As the hail of bullets and mortars intensified, we were all afraid. At the same time each knew his role so well, and was so committed to the others, that fear did not interfere with the clarity and precision with which he directed his actions. There was calm decisiveness with no wasted motion. All of this was enhanced by a trust of the others and a profound respect for the marine infantry; only they could seize and hold the ground the tanks were traversing. Fear was something to be dealt with later, in the privacy of retrospect.

As darkness approached, each crew dug a foxhole, set up a machine gun, and straddled the hole with a tank. We left the escape hatch open so that we could alternate the watch. There were sporadic counterattacks during the night, but the artillery of our 12th Marine batteries kept a steady stream of star shells that illuminated the area. The Japanese had little cover as they charged our lines of fire.

The day that had started for me with an intense experience of cosmic consciousness had rapidly become a series of vignettes offering enlightenment about the parts of the whole, about the resiliency and capacities of human beings for genuine compassion under extreme pressure. Confronted with the fragility of life, I experienced an intense love for the people around me, and a poignant concern for those out there between us and the top of the ridge.

During the next three days it became evident that we would have to pay a high price for victory. The 3d Regiment on our left was engaged in a brutal, bloody battle up the ridges leading to Chonito Cliffs. Colonel Butler ordered me to send our 1st Platoon to reinforce the 3d Marines. Lieutenant Cavender, Warrant Officer Dabbert, Corporal Riebe, the bulldozer driver, and I were able to find routes only part way up Fonte Ridge. The slope soon became too steep for the tanks to climb without our building a road with a pattern of switchbacks. Division headquarters dispatched some engineers and Seabees who demonstrated exceptional resourcefulness and bravery as we followed and covered the 21st Marines yard by hard-earned yard up an incline peppered with Japanese bunkers, caves, and camouflaged nests of soldiers. We used the flamethrower tanks and the bulldozer to bury the caves with ghastly effectiveness.

By the evening of the twenty-fourth, we stood on Mount Tenjo Road at the crest of Fonte Ridge. As we looked across the draw immediately in front of us, we could follow the winding road toward Mount Fonte, where we knew the major battle would have to be fought. General Takashina, the Japanese commander, had no intention of waiting.

For one to understand what happened on the night of 25 July, the morning of the twenty-sixth, it is helpful to know something about the small arms weaponry of the time. Each member of the tank crew was equipped with a .45-caliber pistol, often mistakenly referred to as a "45 automatic." Actually a semiautomatic, it does not fire in bursts. The mechanism must be cocked, and then the slide will place a cartridge in the chamber before the first shot; thereafter, the weapon fires each time the trigger is pressed sufficiently. On firing, the barrel and the slide recoil together, and the slide continues to the rear to eject the spent case and complete the operating cycle. This heavy recoil action makes the weapon notoriously inaccurate. Furthermore, its range is very limited. The most impressive characteristic of a semiautomatic Colt .45 is the devastation the bullet can wreak on any object it hits. Victims of the .45 pistol are seldom wounded; they are obliterated.

During basic training at Quantico we had to become familiar with all weapons and to qualify with three: the rifle (both the Springfield '03 and the M1 Garand), the Browning automatic rifle, and the .45 pistol. Once initiates came to terms with the basic fact that they should press or squeeze rather than pull a trigger, they were well on their way toward qualifying with the rifle. But "pressing" and "squeezing" are not subtle enough descriptions of what is necessary for success with the .45 pistol. With my small hands I had to develop a compensatory strategy.

With a rifle butt fit snugly at the shoulder and the elbow of the supporting arm secured by the rifle sling, the marine was in control at the instant of fire. Recoil was not a real problem. The firing of the second shot was merely a repeat of the first. Anticipating the recoil of the .45 pistol at arm's length, however, was an intimidating experience, and I found that if the instant of fire came as a mild surprise, the tendency to jerk was eliminated and the action much smoother. I visualized myself as a cajoling, enkindling agent and the relationship as one of blandishment. I qualified as marksman with the rifles. The .45 and I attained expert level.

The other critical weapon on the early morning of the twenty-sixth was the hand grenade, a staple among Japanese infantrymen. There was a crucial difference between the American "pineapple" grenade and theirs. Both had four- to five-second delays after the ring was pulled and the igniter activated, but the Japanese grenade had a much higher explosive charge. Unless the latter hit its target with full impact, however, its effectiveness was diminished because the metal casing blasted into fragments much smaller than the more searing American chunks.

On the morning of the twenty-fifth the 3d Marine Division was extended along a nine-thousand-yard frontage on Fonte Ridge. The 3d and 21st Regiments were badly battered, and there were huge gaps in the line, especially between those two regiments. General Turnage pulled Lt. Col. Robert Cushman and his 2d Battalion, 9th Marines, from our right to fill the gap. Because Company B tanks had already climbed the slope, I was assigned to give Colonel Cushman tank support. He was aggressive in securing the exposed flanks of the two regiments and used the tanks extensively. Lieutenant Kirkham and his 3d Platoon actually surrounded and destroyed a Japanese command post and would have proceeded to Mount Fonte on our left, had not one of his tanks struck a land mine. They had also uncovered an enormous supply of sake—which, assuming it was wired, they destroyed. Lieutenant Joy and I brought the headquarters tanks forward and protected Kirkham as the retriever recovered the disabled tank with the crew safely inside. While the operation was well coordinated and effective in closing some of the exposed areas, it was also apparent that the Japanese, rather than retreating, were constantly regrouping. The casualties mounted, and the enemy artillery became more insistent.

At noon I received orders to report back to the commander of the 1st Battalion, 21st Marines, for a reconnaissance mission. Colonel Williams didn't want his men to stay on the ridge: it was too exposed to artillery, and he wanted to move forward as soon as possible. I took Lieutenant Warden, Platoon Sergeants Sprint and Slocum, and two tanks. We determined we could negotiate the shell-pocked road to get around the mangrove swamp directly ahead and support the infantry. We did report, however, many pillboxes, blockhouses, and possible heavy gun sites that were not visible from the ridge. I suggested that the colonel call for artillery barrages in that area. There was also an old quarry in the vicinity that could potentially conceal a sizable force. A radio tower about a mile up the road was still standing; we marveled that it could remain untouched throughout all the bombing and shelling.

The plan was to depart from the ridge at midafternoon and move as far forward as possible until darkness. I called all of the platoon leaders and sergeants for a briefing by Colonel Williams. Lieutenant Warden's 1st Platoon and the headquarters tanks would go with the 2d Battalion, 21st Marines, directly toward the swamp. The 3d Platoon (Lieutenant Kirkham) would go with Company C, 1st Battalion, 21st Marines, as far up the road as they could. Our 2d Platoon (Lieutenant Cavender) would remain in reserve, prepared to protect our left flank.

Just as we were leaving the briefing, the whole area was hit with the most intense enemy artillery and mortar barrages of the entire Guam campaign. Joy and I plunged into one of the larger foxholes just forward of the crest. Lieutenant Warden leaped for one just to our right, but shrapnel tore his right arm severely. Joy and I alternately applied tourniquets made from our undershirts, and Sergeant Slocum ran to my tank to get the morphine that I carried in a first-aid kit. The medical corpsmen trying hard to reach the wounded were overextended. Warden had lost a lot of blood before two corpsmen were able to get him on a stretcher and evacuate him. One detail that seemed of no significance at the time but has stuck in my memory for many years: as the medics started down a trail immediately behind us, they found it too steep and chose another farther to our right.

The 21st Marine's company commanders were anxious to move forward and get as far as they could before dark. After putting Sergeant Slocum in charge of the 1st Platoon, I brought Corporal Panaro and the communications jeep up behind the headquarters tanks so I could maintain contact with Kirkham and the 1st and 2d Battalions.

At 1600 the division commander called for an air strike in the areas we had reconnoitered. Rocket-laden planes were followed by a heavy artillery and mortar barrage as we attacked the ravines and smaller ridges that ringed the swamp. Our tanks fired 75-mm delayed-action high-explosive shells into the ravines directly ahead of the marines. Strong opposition from an interlocking network of caves resulted in many casualties, further depleting the fighting strength of the 21st Marines. And the rain began to pour.

At about 1800 the division dug in for the night on the small ridgeline that we had just secured in front of Fonte Ridge. I assembled the tanks in the draw between the front line and Fonte Ridge, which had been the line of departure. As we were digging foxholes, Colonel Williams sent me a communications corporal who introduced himself as Sparks. Sparks would remain with me to help coordinate the next morning's attack.

The forward companies wanted to move out at daylight, and the corporal would relay my orders during the night. We decided we could best communicate if he, Lieutenant Joy, Corporal Panaro, and I went up Fonte Ridge and set up his equipment behind the draw where the tanks were. Taking my poncho and an undershirt to replace the one I had used as Warden's tourniquet, I headed up the draw. Joy and I chose the foxhole we had occupied during the artillery shelling earlier. Close by, Sparks and Panaro enlarged the one that Lieutenant Warden had tried to reach. Before dark I went down to the draw and told the tank crews to stop digging foxholes, stay in the tanks during the night, and set up some lines of fire for the machine guns and, yes, the 75-mm. We knew there would be counterattacks. I would be in touch with the frontline infantry directly ahead and would relay the situation. These details would make a great deal of difference over the next few hours.

During the early evening, there was an ominous absence of firing. Only yards away could be heard the steady sound of empty sake bottles breaking and taunting yells in Nipponese and broken English. We responded with machine-gun and mortar fire but only sporadically, since there was a real concern about wasting ammunition. We would need it for more definable targets. The enemy began to use flares. With these and our star shells, darkness never came.

At about midnight the enemy unleashed a series of mortar barrages, targeted not only at those of us in forward positions but also at reserve and division headquarters. Sparks received word that enemy patrols were infiltrating his company from all directions. As Panaro and I were relaying this to Radioman Everett Shrock in my tank and to Lieutenant Kirkham and Sergeant Slocum, it became apparent that it was unnecessary. The patrols were charging the tanks, and our machine guns were going full blast. It was also apparent that these Japanese men were much larger than those to whom we were accustomed. There were several attacks, mostly futile, but they did manage to blow one tank's tracks.

At 0400 the shattering of glass intensified, and the panoply of flares and star shells offered a panorama that, at another time and another place, might have been mistaken for a celebration. General

Takashina, however, had chosen this time and this place to launch hundreds of his elite fighting reserve troops—fortified to a frenzy by sake and laden with explosives—against the badly fragmented companies of the 3d Marine Division. It would be the most aggressive confrontation of the campaign.

Breaking through our front line, the Japanese swarmed over and around the tanks. Heedless of the machine-gun fire that was destroying so many of them, they frantically pounded and kicked the tanks and even tried stuffing grenades down the barrels of the 75-mm guns. Hordes bypassed this sector, swarmed down the gulch and up the slope of our ridge. Joy and I had our .45s cocked. Panaro had already started firing his carbine. Sparks was frantically trying to contact his unit, but the radios were carrying another message. He turned to me and shouted, "Captain, let's get the hell out of here! Our artillery is going to pulverize this ridge!"

Joy and the two corporals immediately turned to our right and raced down the path. As I was rising and still on one knee, two Japanese soldiers charged from my left. I aimed the .45 at the chest of the nearest as he came lunging toward me. When the bullet struck, it was as if he were a battered puppet being jerked back over the ridge, his grenade exploding simultaneously. There was no time to waste. I turned to the other and pulled the trigger. Although I was aiming for his chest, the bullet obliterated what was his head while his ignited grenade rolled toward my foxhole. I bolted to my left, but most of the blast caught my chest; I tripped over a body and fell. Then, after scrambling up again, I plunged headlong down the steep path that had daunted Warden's stretcher bearers. The fall saved my life. The 12th Marines' howitzer shells were raining down even before I landed at the bottom of the cliff on a pile of bodies—Japanese and Americans, some dead, many wounded.

I had fallen among the remnants of the Mortar Platoon of the 1st Battalion, 21st Marines, which had been completely overrun by Japanese. As I got up, I felt an excruciating pain on my right side. My undershirt was soaked in blood. I had difficulty breathing. The nagging nausea—the kind of feeling I had always associated with malaria—was extreme. The 2d Platoon of tanks was to my right, firing on the enemy at the convergence of two trails at the foot of the cliff. I cut wide to try to reach Lieutenant Colonel Duplantis's 3d Battalion, which was protecting division headquarters and the field hospital. The artillery and mortar batteries, the shore party units, and all the walking wounded were engaged in close combat with the enemy as its forces savagely charged down the reverse slopes of Fonte Ridge.

By staying close to the riverbank, I entered the 3d Battalion area and reported to Colonel Duplantis. He assigned a young officer to help me establish radio contact with Lieutenant Cavender and my 2d Platoon, which was doing a remarkable job of covering the main enemy entry point to the command area with machine-gun fire. I was able to coordinate their fire with that of a company that Colonel Duplantis wanted to send back up the ridge to reinforce the other battalions.

At about 0600 the sun was bright, the rain had stopped, and General Takashina's coordinated thrust was spent—along with the lives of thirty-five hundred of his very best troops. Lieutenant Joy and I met briefly in front of the division hospital. He had shrapnel in his arm. He did not know what had happened to Panaro or Sparks; they'd been separated by the artillery barrage. The doctors and the medical corpsmen were so overwhelmed with work that I decided that, as long as I could walk, it would be best to join the company going back up the ridge and get to my tanks. A corpsman gave me a clean undershirt. As I washed my chest, I noticed a myriad of small shrapnel fragments and three open wounds. The corpsman covered the affected areas with sulfanilamide powder and dressed the deeper wounds. The bleeding had stopped, although I cut my hands while washing because many of the pieces had not fully penetrated the muscle. I rightly guessed that the pain in my side and my difficulty in breathing were the result of my having broken some ribs in my plunge down the cliff. The corpsman also gave me something for the nausea—a sedative, I supposed.

Between 0900 and noon, evacuation of the wounded and dead was well underway, reorganization of the units was complete, the lines were consolidated, and the coordination between the tanks and infantry was reestablished. Ammunition carriers ceaselessly moved up and down the trails.

At about noon, Col. Hartnoll Withers, the 3d Tank Battalion commander, and Maj. Holly Evans, the executive officer, joined me and Lieutenant Joy on Mount Tenjo Road in front of the ridge to explore the possibility of using all of the tanks as a battalion once we reached the plateau two or so miles ahead. As we talked, Joy pointed to the sky. Flying much higher than any planes we had ever seen were three silver Superfortress B-29s heading westward, eerily silent in the cloudless sky. The new bombers, as it turned out, introduced a new dimension into the war. As he was leaving the ridge, Major Evans insisted I come with him and get some medical attention at the field hospital.

Again, it was a brief stay. A doctor and young corpsman took turns picking grenade fragments out of my chest. They determined that there were three, maybe four, points of real penetration that would require X rays, and perhaps minor surgery, at some later time. They strapped the area around my ribs, and I returned to the ridge.

There were still battles to be fought, but with one or two notable exceptions Japanese resistance became increasingly disorganized, characterized by desperate suicidal charges. One of those exceptions occurred during the tank battalion drive that Colonel Withers had outlined to Holly Evans and me on Mount Tenjo Road. The enemy—led by remnants of their best troops and supported by their remaining heavy artillery and tanks—had fallen back and established a well-fortified position around Finegayan Village astride the road to Mount Santa Rosa. With our Company A in the lead, Colonel Withers commanded a column consisting of tanks, half-tracks, units of the 21st Marines, and two jeeps for communication. After two hours of ferocious attacks and counterattacks, the resistance crumbled, and with tank commanders standing tall in the open turrets, we converged triumphant on the village. I was reminded of General Patton's 3d Army leaving Fort Knox; it was a scene I had never expected to see in the Pacific Theater.

We continued the push until 11 August, when the island was officially declared secure, although it wasn't until twenty-five years later that the last Japanese soldier actually surrendered. In the first twenty-one days after the landing, thousands of American and Japanese youth had been killed or severely wounded. While the statistics are staggering, there are names that remain personally and intensely memorable to me: Schaeffer, Edgecomb, Warden, Miller, Tupper, Long, O'Hara, St. Charles, Raffetto, and Hellman, all severely wounded; Panaro, Prillaman, and Adams, all killed in action. I still carry two fragments in my chest and many more in my mind, including the frightful images of two young Japanese officers dying on Fonte Ridge.

FIVE *Grasping*

Though it is likely that the accusation will annoy you, you are already in fact a potential contemplative: for this act . . . is proper to all men—is, indeed, the characteristic human activity. . . .

And here the practical man, who has been strangely silent during the last stages of our discourse, shakes himself like a terrier which has achieved dry land again after a bath; and asks once more, with a certain explosive violence, his dear old question, "What is the *use* of all this?"

"You have introduced me," he says further, "to some curious states of consciousness, interesting enough in their way; and to a lot of peculiar emotions, many of which are no doubt most valuable to poets and so on. But it is all so remote from daily life. How is it going to fit in with ordinary existence? How, above all, is it all going to help *me*?"

Evelyn Underhill, *Practical Mysticism*

Then dared I hail the Moment fleeing:
"Ah, still delay—thou art so fair!"

Goethe, *Faust*

Even before Guam was declared "secure," and before the engineers and Seabees finished restoring and enlarging the airfields, the battered B-29s were crash landing on returns from raids on the well-defended cities of Japan. The missions were far beyond the range of fighter-plane escorts—a situation that had already determined our next objective.

For the four officers who had gathered on Mount Tenjo Road on 26 July, there would be rapid and significant changes in our roles. Colonel Withers was given command of the 21st Regiment; Major Evans became commander of the 3d Tank Battalion and appointed me as Bn-3 (Battalion Operations Officer), while Joy became commander of Baker Company.

For months, there were guerrilla-type actions in which our weapons of choice were Doberman Pinschers followed by bulldozers and flamethrowing tanks. While some of the Japanese responded to leaflets urging them to surrender, many died of starvation or were killed while making desperate forays into our supply areas in an attempt to steal food. For the operations officers of the division, the situation was an opportunity to train replacements for the next operation while mopping up. Without specifying the exact target, General Erskine, the new division commander, emphasized that our next assault would be against an objective more heavily defended than anything we had yet experienced. That prediction turned out to be no exaggeration.

For me the next five months were terribly busy. Because of the shortage of officers during the initial regrouping, I also served as battalion executive officer and was responsible for the assignment of replacement personnel among the three companies. Captains Stone (Company A) and Lemcke (Company C) were friends of mine, and Quentin Joy (Company B) had been my protégé. While there was intense competition among the companies to acquire combat veterans from among the replacements, especially noncommissioned officers, I made a sincere effort to be objective, and the assignments were generally made in that spirit. Inevitably, however, many close decisions were determined by the luck of the draw.

It was a trying time for me personally. My malaria symptoms, fevers and chills and nausea, did not abate despite heavy doses of quinine. The division medics arranged for me to have an X ray on one of the hospital ships; it confirmed that the three fragments of shrapnel were too deep to remove at the available hospital facilities. However, they were embedded in muscle and therefore posed no immediate risk. It was better to leave them. I had tried to relieve Erna's anxiety about the gravity of the wounds, but distance and imagination magnified her concern. Sensing this, I wrote more frequently and in much greater detail than ever before. Two years apart for loved ones is an inordinately long time. Later she confided that she had been most disconcerted by the type of books I was requesting and had wondered if I were becoming a different person.

Indeed, the events of the six days beginning with 21 July had significantly affected my view of reality. The intense inspirational experience on the morning of the landing was followed by days and nights of increasing angst. There was a clash between my intimations of cosmic unity and the environment of destruction all around me. Though I realize that human beings are not capable of perpetual inspiration, I was not prepared for the depth of melancholy into which I descended over the following months.

It is easy to understand Erna's perplexity over my requests for such esoteric works as Evelyn Underhill's books on mysticism. But if, during those months, such writings were my philosophical and spiritual nourishment, memories of Erna were my emotional sustenance.

The Russo-Japanese War of 1904–5, the catalyst that had uprooted my father at such a young age, was by no means the beginning of the plight of the Lithuanian Jews. Never in their history had the Jews of the Russian Empire been at ease, but with the assassination of Czar Alexander II on 1 March 1881, a wave of pogroms was unleashed against them. It was so virulent that it set in motion great migrations to neighboring European states as well as to America and South Africa.

Although Jews could not own land, my grandfather, Karl Jaffe, and his brother, Wolfe, leased and managed small pieces of farmland. It was a practice that was a vestige of the Council of the Lands administrations during the Middle Ages. In 1894, with the advent of Nicholas II, the last czar, even this arrangement was denied them.

Karl subsisted by teaching, which he had always done parttime. Wolfe, his wife, Ethel, and their twelve children began to emigrate to America in groups, and by 1906 they were all in New York. That family maintained the original spelling of the name Jaffe. When the adolescent Louis arrived and was asked "What's your name?" he answered in his native Russian-Yiddish, "Louis Yaffe." As was so common on Ellis Island, spelling followed phonetics: he became forever Louis *Yaffe.*

While my father maintained little contact with his sister, who had settled in West Virginia, he had even less communication with his cousins in New York. My mother, Fannie, did contact them, and one of the Jaffes visited Sparta on a trip to Florida. After her death, however, there were no more efforts toward reunion among the families.

My father's bad fortunes seemed destined to continue during the 1920s. In 1925 he married again; his wife, Mary, died of cancer within two years of their marriage. Then, when I was nine years old, he married Sarah, who sought to become a mother to me as well as a devoted companion to Louis. She was persistent, also, in reestablishing communications with the Jaffe family in New York. My sister, Rose, and I did visit with members of that family several times during the Depression.

In July 1941 I visited New York. I was already enrolled in the navy's V-5 program and was scheduled to transfer into the Marine Corps the following spring. My father and Sarah, hoping I would delay going into the service, asked me to visit Dora Jaffe Ast in Lakewood, New Jersey. Dora, the oldest of Wolfe Jaffe's daughters, had had special affection for one of Louis's older brothers. She now had a son and daughter, both successful lawyers, and the hope was that I would be inspired to finish law school. That did not occur, but something more fateful did.

On the weekend that I left Dora's home, I visited another Jaffe—Irving, her youngest brother. It was he who had visited Louis and Fannie in Sparta. He took me to the beaches around Sheepshead Bay to play tennis and handball and introduced me to his brother, Max Jaffe, who had a home there. Max also had two daughters, one of whom was eighteen, and Irving felt she would introduce me to some people nearer my own age.

It was late on a Sunday afternoon on Manhattan Beach when I first met Erna. She was with some of her companions. Lithe, vibrant, she had brown eyes that sparkled as she introduced her "lost relative from the South" to her friends. I joined them, and we wove our way through the crowded beaches that were overflowing with enthusiastic people seeking to come within earshot of big bands and entertainers.

Erna and her friends were solicitous of my welfare and fearful of my getting lost. I must have appeared to be lingering, bemused at the scenes cut from this throng. Coming from Sparta I was not accustomed to crowds. No sooner had we reached a spot in front of Vaughn Monroe's orchestra than she took my hand and exclaimed, "Come on, we're going to see the final match of the handball tourney."

I made a mild protest. "I thought the idea was to hear the band."

"No, don't be silly. The idea is to see and taste everything! Come, there's so much more!" Erna's zeal and free-flowing spontaneity pulled us the length of the beaches and back. Toward dusk, we left the beach and went to another part of Brooklyn for supper. Erna insisted that after supper I should spend the night at the Jaffes' home and that she would drive me into Manhattan the following morning. They were all particularly concerned that I have written instructions and a crude map to guide me through the maze of subways and arcane streets of Brooklyn in the event that we were separated on the trains.

We returned about midnight. Erna and I had been attracted to each other when we first met, and we talked until early in the morning. Her exuberance sobered when she talked about my father's isolation from his family. She seemed genuinely concerned about his being stranded in the Deep South. I laughed and assured her that Georgia was not a wilderness and that, in fact, I had been happy growing up there.

"That's not the point." She was emphatic. "You must promise never to be apart from us for so long again."

"With you as the link, I assure you that will never happen," I replied. When she dropped me off at my hotel the next day, the parting was sealed with a kiss that guaranteed that this was not good-bye.

Actually, some twelve months were to elapse before we met again. It was the year when America witnessed the end of the Great Depression, the gearing up of a great world war, and finally our entrance into that conflict. It was a year in which we all drank from the fountain of the future, sometimes with foreboding but always with a frenetic intensity.

The pace of life quickened. While I was in training at Quantico some friends from the V-5 program at Anacostia let me fly with them to various places on weekends. In July 1942 I called Erna and told her I could fly into Floyd Gibbons Airfield on the following Saturday if she could meet me. It was the beginning of six weekends of courtship in Washington, Quantico, and New

York. On Friday, 21 August, I would graduate from officers' training and leave Quantico. With the marines' assault on Guadalcanal on 7 August, we knew that soon I would be leaving the country. As we were preparing for what was to be our last weekend together for the foreseeable future, Erna called and proposed that we marry on Friday.

We had discussed it before. With the certainty that I would be going overseas shortly, I did not feel that our being married would be fair to her. The three or four days preceding the twenty-first were marked by constant telephone conversations between us, interspersed by calls from our parents urging that we marry.

On 21 August 1942 at the home of a justice of the peace in Alexandria, Virginia, Erna and I were married. I had five days of leave before reporting to Camp Lejeune in Jacksonville, North Carolina. We spent three of those days in New York, where there was a wedding celebration on Sunday. In the heaven of cosmic memory I am sure Karl, Wolfe, and their wives, Raisa and Ethel, were shaking their heads and smiling quizzically as they witnessed a hundred and fifty of their descendants with their friends, and some of my U.S. Marine comrades, dancing a *hora* in this first celebratory reunion of the two families since they began to emigrate from Kovno Gibernya, Lithuania, nearly fifty years before. That was their young Louis proudly cutting a slice of the cake.

At Camp Lejeune, I reported to the regimental personnel officer, Captain Kriendler, who was staffing the newly formed 21st Regiment. He spent an inordinate amount of time examining my record from officers' training. He left abruptly and spoke to an aide in an adjoining tent. Upon his return he very matter-of-factly announced, "Yaffe, we have a request for an officer from your class to serve as general's aide in Guantanamo. Your background qualifies you. Only one thing—you'll have to leave in a day or two."

This was something I hadn't anticipated. "Sir, if I don't accept it, how long will I be here?"

He shook his head in disbelief. "Lieutenant, Guantanamo Bay is practically a private beach on the coast of Cuba, and you'd be there at least a year. Everyone here will be on the West Coast in six weeks and in the South Pacific in two, maybe three months. What is it that you really need to know?"

"Sir, I just married last week. I'd like to discuss it with my wife."

"Be here at ten o'clock tomorrow morning with your answer." He closed the file and again shook his head. "And, oh yes, enjoy your evening."

It was a stressful, sleepless evening, and finally Erna and I agreed it would have to be my decision. I reported to Captain Kriendler the following morning that I would decline the duty as general's aide. He impatiently picked up my file again. "We need some officers in a tank battalion that we are just forming. You will report to Captain Evans at the Tank Park."

"The Tank Park?" I queried.

"Yes, it's about ten miles from here. You won't miss it. Lots of mud, the smell of gasoline and diesel fuels, and noise you won't believe. You will never confuse it with the beaches of Cuba, Lieutenant." This was an encounter that Major Kriendler and I recalled sardonically whenever our paths crossed on Guadalcanal, Bougainville, or Guam. He always greeted me by shaking his head in mock disbelief.

Then it all became a blur: scrambling with Holly Evans to build a tank company at New River, North Carolina; rushing to tank tactics school at Fort Knox; speeding cross-country to San Diego; then breathlessly arriving at Camp Pendleton near Oceanside, California, where other tank personnel were converging to form the 3d Tank Battalion. There is, however, one moment, one poignant interlude, that remains sharply etched among these frenetic activities.

My orders from Fort Knox to the West Coast allowed me three days at home in Sparta. It was an opportunity to introduce Erna to my past in the rural South and at the same time to say farewell to my father and Sarah. And others.

Hunt's Hill was a part of Sparta not visited by many white people. I was familiar with it from the many afternoons that Aunt Emma brought me there as she minded her youngest children and grandchildren until the older ones came from school or work. Then she and I would return to my house so that she could prepare supper. Now, as Erna and I approached, her house seemed much smaller than I remembered. The door latch opened tentatively to my knock.

"Mr. Bertram!" It was Sylvia, Aunt Emma's oldest daughter. She was in her forties but seemed much older. "Mama, it's Mr. Bertram!" she called to the next room.

"Sylvia, this is Erna, my wife—" I started, but Aunt Emma didn't give me much time for introductions.

"Come here, boy! Let me give you a hug. Mr. Louie told me you were coming!"

As I moved toward the darkened room, Sylvia grabbed my sleeve and whispered, "You know she's blind—the cataracts and diabetes."

"I know. I'm sorry." Actually, I was apologizing for myself. I had not visited her often enough when I came back during school vacations.

"Come here boy! Give your Aunt Emma a hug! I know you an officer in the army, but you still my little boy!"

She struggled to get out of the huge chair. "You know, I can't move too much. Arthritis, they say."

We embraced. The silver weapons awards on my jacket pressed against her bosom. "What these?" she groped. "You got medals and you ain't been to war?"

"Aunt Emma, this is Erna, my wife."

Emma reached out with both arms. "Come here, child. I got to hug you, too. He's my boy—and that make you my girl."

"Aunt Emma!" Erna fell easily into Emma's embrace.

I guided the aged, bent frame back into her chair. "Tell me, boy, where the army sending you?"

"Actually, Aunt Emma, I'm in the Marine Corps. It's like the navy's army. Erna and I are going to California—way out west." She turned to Erna, who had perched on the arm of Emma's chair. The old woman reached out and touched Erna's head. "What color is her hair, Mr. Bertram?"

"Brown?" Erna answered while looking at me quizzically. We had jokingly differed as to the shading.

"Almost red," I teased as I sat in the chair beside Emma.

"Red! I always warned you about them red-head gals, and here you went and married one." Then Emma turned and felt my arm through the jacket. "You gotten so strong. You still do the push-ups and sit-ups and all that moving around on the floor like you used to?" Still holding my arm, she turned to Erna. "He was so little. His mama and Mr. Louie didn't think he was gonna live. When his mama died, he was such a wee one. All the white folk, and even Mr. Louie, didn't think he was gonna live. But Aunt Emma took this boy, and I said, 'Nothin' gonna happen to this child!'"

She faced me. "You member when I bring that glass of milk and that yeast cake to you at recess every day at school? Quarter to eleven. Quarter to eleven every day." Then back to Erna. "I guess the doctor thought that yeast cake would make him blow up like a cake or a loafa bread."

I explained, "The school was a couple of blocks from our home. Aunt Emma would be there with this glass of milk and a square of raw Fleischman's yeast. We had ongoing baseball games during recess, and all the guys would be standing around yelling 'Finish the milk! Finish the milk! Nobody's covering third base!

Emma, don't fill the glass so full!'" Through the doorway I could see an old piano against the wall in the front room. I asked Sylvia, "Do you still play the piano?"

"I teach my children. I still play the hymns at church."

I addressed Erna. "Sylvia would come to our home with Aunt Emma. My mother had this baby grand piano—you saw it at the house—that she had bought so that her children could take lessons. Sylvia really loved that piano. Aunt Emma made her practice her hymns, but she and I loved jazz. She could hear a tune once and play it right off. We had some records that belonged to my mother. I would wind up the record player, and when the song finished, Sylvia would keep playing the song. She must have done fifty variations on Paul Whiteman's 'Whispering.'" I teased. "Aunt Emma couldn't tell the difference between Sylvia and Whiteman."

She protested. "Aw, I knew what she was doing. I just pretend I didn't." I studied the black face. Despite the wrinkles and a few discolored pink blotches, the smile that I remembered was still wonderfully infectious.

When we finally got up to leave, she faced straight ahead and said simply, "Mr. Bertram, you be careful. If anything happen to you, Mr. Louie couldn't take it."

"I'll be all right, Aunt Emma. I'll write you."

Again, she struggled to rise, and I helped her to stand up. "You don't have to write me. Your daddy and Miss Sarah will let me know when they hear from you. Mr. Louie know how much I love you."

As we embraced, I experienced the fleeting sensation of the love that in my boyhood had insulated me during surges of melancholy and an uncertain feeling of absence and need. And indeed, it was because of Aunt Emma that I could also recall those early years without any real sense of pain.

From Sparta, Erna and I sped to California, where I rejoined Baker Company, now under the command of Capt. Leonard

Reid, who had recently returned from Guadalcanal. He assigned me as the company executive officer.

Erna was my constant traveling companion in those days, but all our activities were driven by my travel orders, my schedules, my nights off, and we really never got to know each other. We lived each day under a sword of Damocles, apprehensively waiting for the order that would ship me out. We took a calculated risk and rented a cottage off base after friends, Lt. George Saussy and his wife, Ginny, showed us the place, at the top of the Laguna overlook, above a cabin that they had rented on the side of the cliff. The cottage belonged to film actors Ida Lupino and Louis Haywood, who would rent it for a minimum of two months, paid in advance. Two months? I didn't know if I would be in the country for two weeks.

Erna was insistent. "Yes!"

A few days after I signed the lease, Captain Reid called the platoon leaders, the warrant officers, and me together. The company would be leaving in ten days. Most of the personnel would embark at San Diego on 15 January, and all leaves would be canceled on 11 January. He turned to me. I was assigned to break camp and, with some tank drivers and maintenance and armament crews, to load all of the tanks, motorized equipment, and heavy weapons on a cargo ship when it was available in two or three weeks.

With the deadline now certain, the pace seemed to slacken. Although the work was intense, Erna and I became more relaxed. The house was idyllic. On the late afternoon of the day that Captain Reid announced the orders, Erna and I started walking down the nearly two hundred wooden steps that followed the side of the bluff to the beach. About half way, we stopped at George and Ginny's hut on the ledge. Lieutenant Saussy was leader of the scout platoon that was attached to our company. He would leave with the first echelon.

Erna and I did not tarry. We were eager to talk to each other and explore things that somehow in the busy four and a half months we had not found time to discuss with seriousness. I was taken aback, initially, by the depth of intelligence and determination that lay beneath her vivacity and childlike playfulness. We were both adamant about my not leaving her pregnant. She wanted to do something for the war effort, perhaps the Red Cross. She would finish college now, so that we could start a family when I returned. At some point, however, she wanted a career of her own. We both assumed I would return to law school.

We strolled the beach and talked for hours. The evening turned cold, and we returned shivering to the steps. As we were passing the hut, Ginny called out. She opened her door and presented us with a large bundle of canvas. "Hey, mates. It gets cold down there. This is our love-making igloo. We won't be needing it for a while. It's great! Enjoy!" Ginny was always bubbly, always perky.

Although being in charge of breaking camp and loading the tanks was a full-time responsibility, I was relieved of night and weekend duty, so that I returned to Erna even when we secured operations after midnight. I would often drive from the docks of San Diego to our house on the cliff, and our dinners would sometimes finish at one or two o'clock in the morning. We didn't mind, even when I had to leave again at dawn. Our time was spent strolling, talking, dining, enjoying Ida Lupino's record collection, and delighting in our spontaneous love-making. Sometimes Erna laughed and reminded me that "you have not been reading your Schopenhauer lately," teasing me about the satchel of books that I always carried. "And I've missed your lectures on Tagore. We're getting carried away."

Erna and I were infatuated with each other from the day we met on Manhattan Beach. On the cliffs overlooking the Pacific in January and February of 1943, we fell in love. When we were apart, she would spend her days strolling and swimming the beaches and writing me letters that were sealed and progressively numbered for shipboard reading.

We finished loading on 11 February. The ship's loading officer informed me that all Marine Corps personnel had to have personal gear aboard the next day. As the senior marine officer, I would assign guard details and grant twenty-four-hour leaves on a daily basis. When I reported aboard on the thirteenth, he told me that the next day I should be prepared to stay. "Be here by 1500."

The early morning of the fourteenth was a time of silence—silently making love, silently strolling the beach, silently having breakfast. We drove to San Diego. Her train to San Francisco would leave at two o'clock in the afternoon. There she would change trains for New York. We would have an early lunch at the Hotel DeSoto, where we had stayed for several days when I reported in from the East Coast.

We were having lunch on the terrace overlooking the city when I suddenly looked up and suggested, "Maybe they have a room available for a couple of hours?"

Erna reverted to her childlike laughter and mischievously challenged me, "I dare you! Let's."

We didn't. But the thought itself was relaxing, and our conversation became less forced. I paid the check, and as we walked down the terrace toward the city by the sea, I stopped abruptly. She was on the step below me. Looking directly into her face, I exclaimed, "I just remembered it!"

Puzzled, she looked up at me. "What?"

"These past few days, I have been trying to remember a line that I wanted to say to you. It's from Goethe's *Faust*."

"And?"

It came easily. "Linger awhile—thou art so fair."

She swallowed and, with a signature gesture of hers, brushed my lips with her fingers. Then she turned quickly and started down the terrace.

During the period on Guam, with an intensity that became an irritant to the company commanders and platoon leaders and strained our friendships, I dedicated myself to applying the tactical lessons I learned during the battle. I scheduled endless small-unit tank-infantry coordination and communication exercises. Since we were going north, we had to prepare for more open terrain and more exposure to antitank weapons. There would be concrete pillboxes and intricate networks of defensive emplacements, different from those encountered in the jungles of the South Pacific and Guam. Coordination with flamethrower and demolition squads took on greater significance and required new tactics. We also had to fire on the move as well as from fixed positions. Having learned that combat requires a flexibility of response that cannot be programmed, I insisted on shifting unit combinations—a practice that the commanders felt impinged on their autonomy.

There is, of course, no such thing as a good war, but no amount of revisionist history has eroded my conviction that from November of 1941 through December of 1945, I was fighting the right war. Hitler's Germany was an evil force that had to be opposed and destroyed. I was fired by the certainty that in doing my assigned part as effectively as possible, lives could be saved, perhaps the war shortened.

I had found a meaningful answer to the apparent polarity between the metaphysical and the practical: the contact with universal life that I was seeking to reestablish could come only by my letting go of my assertive self, by my becoming passive. But was it really possible to surrender to a higher plane of consciousness without self-annihilation? I knew only that, after the intense experience I'd had prior to the assault on Guam, there would not be a day during which I would not—at some period—stand back from the whirl and let intuition quietly have its way with my consciousness.

As we were setting up battalion headquarters, I was able to retrieve my footlocker from the quartermaster's depot area. I was eager to get my books and some periodicals that I had not been able to read in those final weeks of preparation for the assault on Guam. One of the volumes I particularly wanted to read was a compilation of the Hibbert Lectures that Rabindranath Tagore delivered at Manchester College, Oxford, in May 1930. I had found a tattered, secondhand copy for sale from a New Zealand bookseller, and since the work was out of print, I wasn't about to let the opportunity pass. I now skimmed the volume. One of the appendices was a conversation on the nature of reality between Tagore and Albert Einstein on 14 July 1930. The bookseller and I had agreed that this alone was worth the four dollars he charged me. Now, after my conversation with Doc about the tensions among science, philosophy, and spirituality, I wanted to revisit the closing paragraphs of that dialogue. Tagore asserts:

> In the apprehension of truth there is an eternal conflict between the universal human mind and the same mind confined in the individual. The perpetual process of reconciliation is being carried on in our science and philosophy, and in our ethics. In any case, if there be any truth absolutely unrelated to humanity then for us it is absolutely non-existing.
>
> It is not difficult to imagine a mind to which the sequence of things happens not in space, but only in time like the sequence of notes in music. For such a mind its conception of reality is akin to the musical reality in which Pythagorean geometry can have no meaning. There is the reality of paper, infinitely different from the reality of literature. For the kind of mind possessed by the moth, which eats that paper, literature is absolutely

non-existent, yet for Man's mind literature has a greater value of truth than the paper itself. In a similar manner, if there be some truth which has no sensuous or rational relation to the human mind it will ever remain as nothing so long as we remain human beings.

Einstein replies: "Then I am more religious than you are!"

I wanted to write Erna about this! It would bring a smile of remembrance of our days on the cliff above Laguna and her teasing about my "lectures on Tagore."

In November, General Erskine led a concerted sweep of the island to gather up the remaining Japanese and eliminate any threat of guerrilla actions. While it netted only a hundred or so soldiers, we all knew that the purpose was to clear our minds for what was ahead. The following week the regimental and battalion commanders along with the operations officers were called to division headquarters for a briefing by Intelligence on our next operation. The two lieutenants in charge of the briefing were describing a small rock of an island and seemed confused as to whether it belonged to the Bonin or the Volcano group. They did know, however, the name of the island—Iwo Jima. It was only 660 miles from Tokyo.

six Nausea

For meritorious achievement in the performance of his duties while serving as operations officer of a Marine tank battalion prior to and during the operations on Iwo Jima, Volcano Islands, from 7 November 1944 to 27 March 1945. During the planning and training phases from 7 November 1944 to 12 February 1945, Captain Yaffe displayed exceptional ability in organizing, training, and preparing the battalion for the proposed operation. The development of, and training for, tank-infantry teamwork achieved a greater emphasis and state of efficiency under his guidance than ever before realized among the units of the division. During the operations from 23 February to 20 March 1945, he untiringly devoted himself to his tasks; submitted plans for the solving of many complex problems; and executed his commanding officer's decisions thereon with exceptional determination and skill. By his personal courage, example, and professional ability, he was instrumental in the success of a most difficult operation. His conduct throughout was in keeping with the highest traditions of the United States Naval Service.

Lt. Gen. Roy S. Geiger, USMC, awarding the Gold Star in lieu of a second Bronze Star

Half a century later it all comes back as a melange of sights, sounds, and temperatures. Bougainville bursts into a pageant of color, vibrant with rapidly growing vegetation. Guam brings to mind a thunderous cacophony after which an instant of silence is the defining event. But with Iwo, beyond the intermingled sights and sounds, there is the omnipresent chill of my mind and body. The landscape is draped in ever-darkening shades of gray, some bordering on black, and all sounds are muffled except a persistent, not-so-distant thunder. I can almost see the bleak tone of the wind at Iwo. I can still hear the searing thuds of gray on blackened volcanic ash followed by streaks, then floods, of crimson from body parts, detached fragments of arms, legs, faces.

On 28 March 1945, a day after I returned to Guam from Iwo Jima, I was called to report to Lt. Col. Arthur Butler, division operations officer. All of the 3d Marine Division personnel who had served in the three campaigns were to be rotated and sent back to the States for at least six months. He had been told that within a few days I would be among the first officers to leave. Would I stay, he asked, and translate the Tank Battalion diary into an official account and help integrate it into the division's Special Action Report?

Colonel Butler had been in the advance echelon of every important action of the division, and I had served with him on many of those assaults. When I put a face on the legendary image of the quiet, resourceful, decisive marine commander, I think of Colonel Butler.

"Colonel, I'm tired. I really don't feel well. I'd like to go home."

I think he smiled. "I know."

We talked about Iwo for a while.

While it seemed ridiculous that a pork chop–shaped island only five miles long and two and one-half miles at its widest point, east to west, could merit the lives and resources lavished on it, the military importance of Iwo was immense. Its radar gave early warning of the B-29 raids that were the prelude to America's final assault on the Japanese homeland. The island possessed two airstrips and a third under construction. From these bases, Japanese fighter planes were taking a frightful toll on U.S. bombers and costing dearly in American lives. Also from here the enemy was sending out bombing forays against Guam and Tinian.

We wanted Iwo as a base for American fighter craft to protect B-29s during the final assaults. For this reason, in little over a month 6,821 American marines and navy personnel were killed, another twenty-two thousand wounded, and there were twenty-two thousand Japanese casualties. In savagery of firepower and bloodletting, the Battle of Iwo Jima surpassed Normandy, Anzio, Tarawa, and all battles since Gettysburg. Colonel Butler and I speculated on the number of our crippled bombers that would be landing before we even secured the island. Speculation on the number of lives saved was most reassuring to both of us. "We didn't float in reserve very long," he noted wryly.

The V Amphibious Corps was the assault force designated to take Iwo Jima. It was comprised of the 3d, 4th, and 5th Marine Divisions, each with twenty-one thousand men, including tank, artillery, and engineer battalions plus ten thousand navy and Seabee personnel. The 4th and 5th would land on a thirty-five-hundred-yard strip of beach that started near the foot of Mount Suribachi and extended up the eastern side of the island. No more units could be accommodated on the beachhead. The 3d Division would remain in floating reserve fifty or sixty miles at sea—not for use now, it was hoped, but in preparation for the next operation, which, we found out later, would be Okinawa.

"Colonel, how long do you think it'll take—these reports?"

"About two weeks, more or less."

"Going well into my third year away, I guess I can stand a couple of weeks more. If I can help, I'll stay."

As I was leaving he stood up and laughed. "You made a good choice. When we've finished, I'll see to it that you fly out of here. You'll be home long before the others."

I'm sure the look on my face was quizzical enough to prompt a response. "Yeah, I didn't want that to influence your decision."

The paper is parched and faded, but it stirs up keen memories. I vividly recall a sulfuric smell. . . .

C O N F I D E N T I A L
Headquarters, 3d Tank Battalion,
3d Marine Division, Fleet Marine Force
c/o Fleet Post Office, San Francisco
Special Action Report—Iwo Jima

Part I. Summary: 7 November 1944–27 March 1945
A. 1. This report covers the 3d Tank Battalion's activities in planning, training, logistical preparation, and embarkation relative to the Iwo Jima Operation for the period 7 November 1944 to 12 February 1945.

2. This report includes a narrative résumé of this unit's activities en route to, and while on the objective for this period 12 February 1945 to 22 March 1945.

3. This report further contains a "play by play" narrative of important events from the beginning of this battalion's action to reembarkation for the period 23 February 1945 to 27 March 1945.

B. Narrative Summary
1. The 3d Tank Battalion, having begun embarkation on 12 February 1945, was completely embarked upon 2 LSTs and 2 AKAs [attack cargo ships] by 16 February. All convoys sailed that date.

Maps were issued and officers and men were briefed as thoroughly as possible on all aspects of the operation.

On 21 February the LST convoy was attacked by a squadron of "suicide bombers" just off Minami Iwo, and LST 477 was "rammed" about fifteen feet aft of the starboard magazine, bomb and plane penetrating into the tank deck. This unit suffered three men killed, ten wounded, and various tank equipment damages.

* * *

You could not get close to Iwo without being involved in the carnage. I was on LST 477.

The LST is a three-hundred-foot flat-bottomed craft designed to carry cargo, vehicles, and assault troops ashore. The bow ramp opens and belches forth equipment and personnel onto the beach ready for action. Beyond that critical utility, its chief disadvantage is its vulnerability to enemy fire, especially low-flying aircraft. Slow and clumsy in maneuver, its only defenses in World War II were four, sometimes six, batteries of 40-mm antiaircraft weapons. Marines aboard LSTs had a special reverence for antiaircraft crews.

The assault tanks and crews were on LSTs 477 and 646. Maj. Holly Evans, who was the battalion commander, and I were on LST 477 with Able Company, part of Charlie Company and some Headquarters personnel. As operations officer I had a staff of three: Lts. Louis Spiller and Jim Gindreaux and SSgt. Robert Mann. Lou Spiller had served with me in Baker Company and had received a field promotion after the Battle of Guam. Sergeant Mann was with me; the two lieutenants were on LST 646 with B Company and the remainder of C and Headquarters Companies under Capt. Gerald Foster, who had recently arrived from the States and served as battalion executive officer.

On the evening of 16 February we joined the seventy-two-mile-long convoy of ships, men, and weaponry bearing down on Iwo for D day, 19 February. We were to be the final movement in a symphony of destruction, fearful in both its simplicity and confinement of theater. The cacophony had begun seventy-two days before, with high-level B-24 bombings and sporadic, piercing dive-bombing attacks. The fury became more insistent with the bass of shattering naval gunfire and, weather permitting, more medium-level bombings and rocket assaults. All available instruments of explosive destruction were culled from the continents and the vast Pacific and focused on the eight square miles of an extinct volcanic mountain top rising from the sea, a desolate place from which the only visible activity was a miasma of rising sulfurous mist. The labyrinthine caves and crags and concrete networks of emplacements, however, contained much more.

In the radio room of the LST, Major Evans and I established communication with the 3d Marine Division staff. He and I then took turns briefing groups of officers and tank commanders on the initial battle plans, the terrain, and the objectives for D day through D plus 3. The island was small enough to be divided into thousand-yard grids, a total of thirty-three numbered squares on our maps. Stretching from Mount Suribachi's base north were three successive steps of plateau, each rising abruptly above the lower and each containing an airstrip—Motoyama airfields 1, 2, and 3. Between airfields 2 and 3 were the bombed remains of Motoyama Village. This was the island of Iwo Jima.

On 17 February, Colonel Butler alerted us to the possibility that our tank battalion might be called before the main force of the 3d Division if the casualties of the 4th and 5th Tank Battalions became too great. Our LSTs were ordered to be within twenty to thirty miles offshore on D day.

The three days prior to D day were mostly rainy and cold, with a stream of squalls that made all the marines and nearly all the sailors seasick. Most of us had been in the South Pacific for two years, and the 40-degree temperature added to the discomfort. The weather also hampered the naval bombardment and the effectiveness of the marine pilots' Corsairs.

On 17 February, while monitoring the situation in the communications room, we picked up some frantic, random messages from a flotilla of rocket-firing gunboats. They were drawing direct artillery fire from the Japanese, who mistakenly thought they were advance units of the invasion. Most of the gunboats were destroyed, and two hundred men were killed, wounded, or drowned in just over an hour. While it may have been one of the very few tactical mistakes on the part of General Kuribayashi—it exposed some of his heavy artillery positions, which our fleet immediately attacked—it cast a pall over our invasion force that not even the improved weather could lift.

On D day the weather was good, and most of us were on deck at sunrise. At 0630 Adm. Kelly Turner gave the order: "Land the landing force." H hour was 0900, and we were thinking of the men of the 4th and 5th Divisions who had been up for hours and had long ago pushed aside unfinished plates of steak and scrambled eggs. No matter how palatable it is, one doesn't relish food on the morning of D day.

Though our LST was over twenty miles from the island, we were on the fringe of an armada of battleships, cruisers, destroyers, LSTs, and attack transports engaged in thunderous shelling and bombing. The assault waves would land in amphibian tractors (AMTRACs) rolling out of the mouths of LSTs, with Higgins boats loaded with marines following. Next, LSTs carrying tanks would discharge their cargo as securely as the surf and terrain would allow. We knew the tanks would have problems negotiating the black volcanic sand as well as the steep, ten- to fifteen-feet-high terraces that began only yards inland. Here the infantry, engineers, and Seabees would have to lead us. We had developed a tactic of repeatedly laying yards of iron-meshed mats and moving small distances so that the tank tracks would not sink into the soft earth. It had worked on the coral beaches. We didn't really know what would happen in volcanic ash, however.

At about 0700 Maj. Holly Evans, Capt. Bill Stone (Able Company Commander), and I went to the communications cubicle where I had spread out the maps. From an overlay, I marked off the objectives for the first three days. We silently gazed at numbered grids that we had memorized thoroughly. There wasn't much to talk about.

"Let's get some coffee," Holly suggested.

For three days I subsisted on coffee and cigarettes. I did not know if the incessant nausea was from malaria or seasickness, but I suspected it would have persisted if I had had neither of these problems. As we approached the officers' mess, I went to the head and went through my ritual retching, though there was nothing to bring up. Still, it gave me temporary relief when I followed it with coffee.

As I was going to the mess hall, I passed WO Martin Newton talking to some men from Able Company.

"Do we know anything, Cap'n?"

"We won't know anything before noon," I replied. "Why are you wearing that life jacket?"

"Are you kidding? I'll be sleeping in this thing from here on in." I may have smiled, but I doubt it.

I looked at the men from Able Company. "Captain Stone is with me. He'll know the minute I know anything. I'm sure you guys are ready."

One of them laughed. "Not really."

They all laughed. There wasn't much else to do.

This time, the coffee didn't help. I had to leave the smoke-filled officers' mess and walk to the bow of the boat. The antiaircraft crews were intent on the skies and the horizon. The marines' eyes were glued on the port side where, even from this distance, we could see the spiraling smoke rising as sixteen-inch shells from the battleships pulverized the island.

Shortly after eight o'clock the thunder ceased. I was puzzled; this was too early for the silence that I had anticipated would arrive at about fifteen minutes before H hour. The gunnery crews pointed skyward to the east. The sky was filled with carrier-based Corsairs, fighter planes, and bombers. Within minutes, rockets, bombs, and strafing reached an ear-piercing crescendo.

Sergeant Mann came over at about 0830 and told me the skipper of the LST was picking up scattered messages that I might want to hear. I told Bob to get Major Evans and Captain Stone and to join us all in the communications room. Most of the messages were just communication checks from the AMTRACs and the 4th and 5th Tank Battalion tanks. We were anxious to know if they were drawing artillery fire from the volcanic bastion. Apparently not.

A few minutes before 0900, I left the communications cubicle and again started toward the head. As I reached the main deck, I was suddenly aware that the bombing had ceased; the silence had set in. I didn't have time to reach the head; I went to the nearest railing to puke.

The entire landing area for the two assault divisions was less than two miles long and, in ironic contrast to the actual ashen terrain, the seven beaches were named "green," "red" 1 and 2, "yellow" 1 and 2, and "blue" 1 and 2, a few hundred yards to each. The 5th Division landed on the green and red beaches to the south at the foot of Mount Suribachi. The 4th Division had the four yellow and blue beaches to secure, push inland and turn north to take airfield 1. The 5th Division's objective was to push straight ahead to choke the island at its narrowest part (about a half-mile across) while at the same time turning south to assault Mount Suribachi. The objective on D day was to neutralize Suribachi and secure Motoyama airfield 1. Certainly two marine divisions would be able to handle the expected counterattacks.

The Japanese never doubted that Iwo would be an essential objective for the American assault on Japan. With its heavy antiaircraft defenses forcing our B-29s into wide detours on missions to Japan, and as a point of origination for air raids against our staging areas, control of the Volcano Islands was key to an assault on the enemy's homeland. In 1944 Emperor Hirohito personally chose Lt. Gen. Tadamichi Kuribayashi to command the defense of this stronghold that had been building for nearly two years. He also gave him twenty-four thousand seasoned troops. These units were supported by vast resources of artillery, huge rockets, 329-mm and 81-mm mortars, and antitank units, all inter-connected and controlled by underground telephone cables. Smaller mortars were carefully concealed and so strategically placed that one soldier could feed shells into several weapons at the same time. The precise registration over the area for artillery and mortar shells was such that no invading marine could remain in one spot very long.

There was even more—much more—weaponry in the bastion's arsenal. General Kuribayashi had devised an intricate network of steel and concrete bunkers connected by tunnels to withstand the initial bombardment. There were hundreds of blockhouses, pill-boxes, and caves with satellite emplacements for machine guns with fields of interlocking fire to cover every approach from the shallow landing areas of the beaches. With mortars and artillery added to these, the Japanese were literally behind a wall of fire, and they had commanding positions from the top of five-hundred-and-fifty-foot Mount Suribachi, on the southernmost tip of the island, as well as from the hills surrounding Motoyama airfield 2.

General Kuribayashi had no intention of throwing his men against marines supported by enormous naval gunfire. His strat-egy was to let enough marines land to fill the beaches with men ankle-deep and vehicles churning ever deeper in the grasping vol-canic sand. For an hour, marines swarmed onto the black, clut-tered landing strip while the Japanese unleashed their deadly machine-gun crossfires and a few mortars when the invaders tried to mount the terraces and hummocks bounding the few yards of beach front.

Then General Kuribayashi lit the torch, and the wall of fire came down.

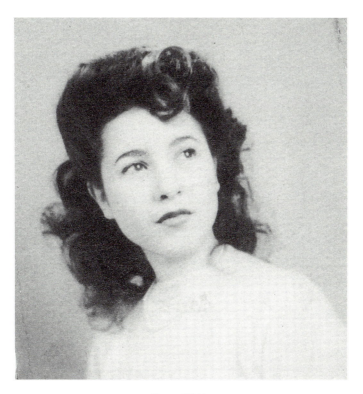

Erna, 1941.

Author and Erna celebrating their wedding, August 1942.

Introduction to tanks, Camp Lejeune, 1942. Pfc. Elmer Kanocz, *left,* and Cpl. Thomas Slocum. *Courtesy Tom Murphy*

Building a crew, Camp Lejeune, 1942. *Left to right:* Harry Trefsgar, Costanzo Trapani, Leroy Conroy. *Courtesy Tom Murphy*

The death of Lt. Leon Stanley. In the dense jungles of Bougainville a marine patrol with scout dogs identify a Japanese machine gun emplacement and calls for tank support. Lt. Stanley's tank is disabled by a land mine and he is shot in the head as he attempts to abandon the vehicle. He is lying on the ground beside the tank. *U.S. Marine Corps photo*

Members of the scout patrol open fire on the enemy soldiers who killed Stanley and this brings fire from the Japanese machine guns. *U.S. Marine Corps photo*

Pfc. R. E. Lansley seeks cover from machine gun fire. Once he reaches safety the tanks open fire and demolish the Japanese emplacement. *U.S. Marine Corps photo*

Members of the patrol administer first aid while the rest of the patrol, under the protection of the tanks, takes over the enemy position. Nineteen Japanese soldiers, including the one who shot Lt. Stanley, were killed in this encounter. *U.S. Marine Corps photo*

Marines and Seabees take charge, 1943. *Courtesy Walter Roose*

Taking territory and trophies, Bougainville, 1943. *Left to right:* author, Lt. Lemcke, and Lt. Rudd.

Preparing for Guam, May 1944. Members of Company B, 3d Tanks, on maneuvers on islet of Rua Sura off Guadalcanal. *Courtesy Walter Roose*

Tank at Finegayan. *U.S. Marine Corps photo*

Tanks and infantry coordinate on Guam. *U.S. Marine Corps photo*

Officers of Company B, 1944. *Kneeling:* Lt. Kirkham, author, W. O. Riley. *Standing:* Lt. Warden, Lt. Joy, Lt. Cavender.

Tanks heading for Motoyama Airfield No. 2, Iwo Jima. *U.S. Marine Corps photo*

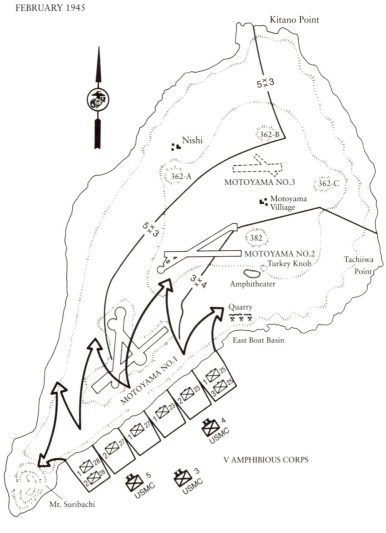

THE ASSAULT ON
IWO JIMA
FEBRUARY 1945

Kitano Point

5 ✕ 3

Nishi

362-B

362-A

MOTOYAMA NO.3

362-C

Motoyama
Villiage

5 ✕ 3

382

MOTOYAMA NO.2

Turkey Knob

Tachiiwa
Point

3 ✕ 4

Amphitheater

Quarry

East Boat Basin

MOTOYAMA NO.1

1 ✕ 25
3 ✕ 25

2 ✕ 23
3 ✕ 23

1 ✕ 27

4
USMC

V AMPHIBIOUS CORPS

2 ✕ 27

1 ✕ 28
2 ✕ 28

5
USMC

3
USMC

Mt. Suribachi

1000   0   1000   2000

YARDS

Major Holly Evans awards Purple Hearts to *(from left)* Lt. Quentin Joy, Capt. William Stone, author, and Lt. Charles Kirkham. Guam, 1944.

Author, June 1945.

From Suribachi to San Francisco. The author *(second from left)* and three other marines celebrate their first night back in the states. April 1945.

Starting a family. Erna, Erich, and the author, 1946.

SEVEN The Divine Wind

A rocky mountain-top, within sight of the sea.

Enter STRENGTH *and* VIOLENCE, *dragging in*
PROMETHEUS. HEPHAESTUS *follows.*

STRENGTH: Here we have reached the remotest region
    of the earth,
The haunt of Scythians, a wilderness without a footprint.
Hephaestus, do your duty. Remember what command
The Father laid on you. Here is Prometheus, the rebel:
Nail him to the rock; secure him on this towering summit
Fast in the unyielding grip of adamantine chains.
It was your treasure that he stole, the flowery splendour
Of all-fashioning fire, and gave to men—an offence
Intolerable to the gods, for which he now must suffer,
Till he be taught to accept the sovereignty of Zeus
And cease acting as champion of the human race.

Aeschylus, *Prometheus Bound*

Prometheus was condemned to suffer continuously throughout eternity as punishment for having given mankind the stolen gift of fire. If the gods had commanded a performance of their cosmic tragedy in February of 1945, Prometheus would surely have been bound to Mount Suribachi on Iwo Jima. Aboard ship we grasped the chaos and some of the horror from cryptic, frantic messages sifted through static from company command posts as the avalanche of artillery and whirring mortar shells fell among the assault waves. Other descriptions came randomly from observation aircraft. Bomb craters that had been sought for shelter became pits of torn bodies, those still alive crying, "Corpsman! Corpsman!! Corpsman!!" But corpsmen, too, were trapped.

Throughout the afternoon many things became increasingly and painfully clear, even from our distance. The myriad of powerful, rapid-firing Japanese antiaircraft batteries, so strangely silent during the last few days of the preinvasion B-24 bombings, had not been silenced by our naval barrages. We had been too optimistic. With deadly accuracy the Japanese were now level-firing on craft bringing tanks and artillery support for the regimental combat teams. Many tanks and AMTRACs sank with their crews in the raging surf. Others escaped, only to be destroyed by blasting land mines.

Valor, indeed, was a common virtue among these marines. Passing among fallen comrades, they carried satchels of explosives, pole charges, and flamethrowers and advanced through hummocks filled with enemy who were firing automatic weapons onto a moonscape of ravines and caves. Covering one another, the marines identified targets for bazookas and those tanks that had made it ashore. At the end of the day, though far short of their objective, thirty thousand marines were on Iwo, and they meant to stay.

By late afternoon no one on LST 477 doubted that we would be called. During the night, our skipper received orders to move the ship to within three miles of the island. On Iwo, the expected banzai counterattacks never came—only the ceaseless inferno of General Kuribayashi's wall of fire and the tortured screams of maimed marines, strong because the voices were so young.

By dawn of D plus 1, twenty-four hundred marines were either dead or being ferried to the overwhelmed naval surgeons aboard the hospital ships *Samaritan* and *Solace*. Despite terrible losses, the 28th Regimental Combat Team (RCT) of the 5th Division surrounded the base of Mount Suribachi on the southern flank, and the 23d RCT straddled the narrow neck of the island at the base of the volcano. The 4th Division, RCTs 24 and 25, reached the edge of airstrip 1 and now faced a bloody yard-by-yard battle north through the determined enemy. Every yard taken revealed how well-camouflaged the defense positions were and how little damage the intensive bombardment had inflicted on the intricate network of concrete and steel emplacements.

At noon we received an alert from division headquarters: the 3d Tank Battalion and the 21st Marine Regiment would land on Iwo as soon as there was room on the beach. In the meantime LST 477 would return to the rendezvous area, about thirty miles at sea. This order disturbed the navy crew. Throughout the whole invasion the sailors' concern had been the dreaded kamikazes, the elite corps of suicidal dive-bomber pilots. The name signifies "divine wind," a monstrous typhoon that destroyed a Mongol fleet invading Japan in 1281. We knew the Japanese were amassing thousands of obsolete "Zero" (Mitsubishi A6M2, later codenamed "Zeke") and "Betty" (Mitsubishi G4M2) bombers armed with torpedoes, bombs, and only enough fuel to get to the targets— American carriers, escort carriers, and other vital ships, vessels like those circling the area to which we were headed.

I put on my life jacket and carried my helmet as I joined Warrant Officer Newton for coffee in the officers' mess. He nodded toward my jacket and smiled.

"You're finally getting the hang of it."

I had enormous respect for the marine warrant officers. Generally they were older than most of us and had achieved their rank through some special expertise. I particularly appreciated Martin Newton, whose knowledge of weaponry was immense. Tall, lean, in his very early thirties, Newton was quiet and low-keyed except when the discussion focused on some phase of gunnery. Then he became animated, his hazel eyes sparkling and his thin mustache accentuating a ready smile. Newt loved the wonders of technology. He and I had become friendly in the high country of northern New Zealand when he helped me build a firing range for the tanks of Company B. Later he and Warrant Officer Dabbert were indispensable as we shed the Stuart tanks with their 37-mm guns and became a company of Shermans armed with formidable 75-mms. Aboard LST 477, Newton was consumed with the navy's rapid-firing 40-mm antiaircraft batteries and spent much of his time observing them.

That day, D plus 1, Newt wasn't happy. He shook his head. "The problem is, it isn't enough to hit the damn kamikazes. You have to *destroy* them. They're so fuckin' close and low and on a direct line for you. Even if you hit the bastard, he can still take you with him. That's what he came for."

He took a deep drag on his cigarette and nodded toward the open port. "Look at that horizon. The sonofabitch comes in at that level—twenty or thirty feet off the water. I'm not even sure we can depress those 40-mms to that angle. Besides, look at all those fuckin' boats out there. We'll be shooting at *them*, and they'll be shooting at *us*."

Major Evans joined us and showed me a message from D-3 (our division operations section). The 21st Marines had received orders to disembark, but the navy had closed down the beach. The surf was too high, and enemy shelling on the beach was unabated.

As I got up, I assured Newt, "Tomorrow you won't have to worry about kamikazes." I was wrong.

On 21 February, D plus 2, the winds were strong, the rain was torrential, and the surf high. All that plus the clutter made further reinforcements impossible for most of the day. Despite the weather, however, the carrier-based planes pummeled Suribachi and the northern hills with napalm. Suffering enormous casualties, the 4th and 5th Divisions inched forward and controlled most of airstrip 1. Although fresh troops and more tanks were needed, the 21st Regiment of the 3d Marine Division spent seasick hours circling the line of departure in Higgins boats, waiting for the beach to open up.

On LST 477 there were several air alerts—our radar men were having difficulty distinguishing between our own planes returning to the carriers and those that belonged to the enemy. At each alert, the marines went to their bunks to get out of the way of the navy personnel. Major Evans and I went to the communications area; Captain Stone, the platoon leaders, and most of the warrant officers went to the officers' mess adjoining the radio room.

The 21st Regiment, under Colonel Withers, finally got ashore by late afternoon and was assigned to the 4th Division. They also needed more tanks, but there was no room for them on the beach. At about five o'clock we received word that we would have orders to land the next day. Again there was nothing for us to do but to drink coffee, think about tomorrow, retch, and circle the big navy ships.

At 1830, however, all that changed. The Japanese had located our naval task force and, from the southern home islands, unleashed successive waves of kamikaze bombers and fighter planes. The radar on the destroyers and the returning Corsairs picked up the first wave at sundown, and red alerts flashed frantically on all the boats. General quarters sounded as we scurried for battle stations.

Suddenly rolls of fiery smoke rose from the carrier *Saratoga* and some of the other ships. A wall of antiaircraft fire enveloped the area, punctuated with flaming kamikazes crashing into the sea or into secondary targets. LST 477 was a secondary target. Both of our starboard antiaircraft crews picked up two kamikazes coming just off the water and fired. One of the planes disintegrated into a flaming ball. The other, also flaming, crashed and exploded into our 40-mm battery, killing the entire crew. The blast triggered a series of tremendous explosions among the ammunition lockers; flames and debris spurted a hundred feet into the air. The damage-control crew moved quickly and bravely into the area, but not before the eruptions had killed six sailors and three marines and wounded four other navy crewmen in the compartment immediately beneath the battery. Two more planes crashed into a mine sweeper a few hundred yards west.

The marines below rushed topside despite the hails of shrapnel shooting everywhere across the deck. We were accustomed to having a job to do during combat. A defined role pushed much of the fear aside. But here, under siege aboard ship, we felt the fright of having to stand by, helpless. Soon singly and then in small groups, the marines—including officers—moved to help man the fire-fighting equipment, sweep burning debris off the deck, and improvise stretchers to move the wounded to shelter. Warrant Officer Newton directed some of our tank gunners to follow him, and they hovered around the remaining 40-mm batteries, doing whatever they could to help.

The blowups shorted the power lines. Just as the flames approached the forward magazine, the pumps failed and there was no pressure in the water mains that supplied the hoses needed to wet down the ammunition. The ship's engines were silent. The LST was helpless in the water.

Motor Machinist Mate Blaine Heinze and Electrician's Mate Keith McCammen, with cool determination and ingenuity, crawled down to the burning forward tank-deck, over heaps of hot ammunition, ran jumpers around the frayed electrical circuits, and returned power to the lines. Within minutes the hoses began blasting water at the blaze, and the ship was again able to maneuver.

The attack lasted only about thirty minutes. There were, we later learned, fifty kamikaze planes. They sank the escort carrier *Bismarck Sea* and severely crippled the *Saratoga* as well as many of their secondary targets.

Warrant Officer Newton and I joined Lt. Joseph Cowden, a ship's officer, and inquired about casualties. Besides our obvious concern about the marines, Newt had come to know the 40-mm crews very well. "It's too early for a report," the lieutenant said. He then pointed to the bridge. "It was amazing how they came in so close without being detected. A lookout reported planes in the clouds, and almost before he finished the words, they were here. The leader passed our bridge so close he would have been an easy target for a baseball."

We spent the night down on the tank deck assessing the damage to the tanks. Fortunately the gaping hole was several feet above the waterline, but it still presented a major problem. The explosion had jammed the huge starboard door that had to swing open before the landing ramp could be lowered, and three of the vehicles were damaged badly. Maintenance crews worked throughout the night while we listened apprehensively for condition-red alerts.

"We didn't sign up for this," Martin Newton groaned. "I don't care what's happening on that damned beach. Let's get the hell offa here."

EIGHT *Gasping*

24 February

At 2230 received orders to [have one company of tanks] proceed to 164D (North end of Airfield No. 1); "A" Company arrived at 2400 and remained in position remainder of night, so as to be available for support of 9th RCT on the following morning.

**Special Action Report, 3d Tank Battalion,
3d Marine Division, April 1945**

There is the reality of paper, infinitely different from the reality of literature. For the kind of mind possessed by the moth, which eats that paper, literature is absolutely non-existent, yet for Man's mind literature has a greater value of truth than the paper itself.

**Rabindranath Tagore, conversation with
Albert Einstein, 14 July 1930**

Tagore's distinction between realities is valid for any written word or communication. That entry in the report—what moths, time, and humidity have spared—is sufficient to evoke an appalling chill. The hour and a half between 2230 and 2400 on D plus 5 remains for me a period fraught with a terror beyond any I have ever experienced.

The 3d Marine Division, one of three divisions of the V Amphibious Corps, joined combat on the island of Iwo Jima late in the day of D plus 2, 21 February, when the 21st RCT under Col. Hartnoll Withers finally landed, despite the fury of the surf and the continuous, brutal mortar and artillery fire on the beach. Withers's mission was to relieve the badly battered 23d Marines of the 4th Division, continue forward to secure Motoyama airfield 1, and gain a foothold on what was turning out to be the impenetrable airfield 2. Casualties mounted even as his troops moved into positions between the terraces above the beach and the revetments beneath the first airfield. It would get worse.

Our tanks were badly needed. The LSTs beached under the cover of darkness during the night of 22 February, and LST 646 discharged tanks early on the morning of D plus 4. These twenty-five tanks from B and C Companies reported to the corps commander for action with the 4th and 5th Tank Battalions. Because of the kamikaze damage on LST 477, we could neither open our starboard door nor lower the ramp. Three Sherman tanks were damaged.

As we worked frantically with acetylene torches to free the mammoth door of the ship, mortar shells rained down from Suribachi. Although the 28th Marines kept constant pressure on the Japanese and the mortar fire seemed increasingly random, the mayhem on the beach continued relentlessly. At about 0900 a crewman from the port antiaircraft battery motioned to me and excitedly offered me his binoculars. He pointed to Suribachi: a platoon of marines was working its way up a path to the summit. This was indeed good news.

An hour and a half later, suddenly there were flashings of ships' lights, soundings of sirens, clanking of bells, and shouts from marines and sailors. The radios were signaling: "The flag is on Suribachi! The flag is raised!" This was the awe-inspiring moment captured in a photograph by *Leatherneck* staff photographer Louis Lowery. Later that day the scene was recaptured with a larger flag in the unforgettable shot by Associated Press photographer Joe Rosenthal. It would become the most famous photograph of World War II.

Meanwhile the battalion sergeant major along with Lts. Lou Spiller and Jim Gindreaux had established our battalion headquarters. They had removed the bodies from two Japanese bunkers that had been neutralized by tank flamethrowers and demolition teams. By early afternoon we had unloaded the tanks from our LST and, with the aid of meshed-steel matting, began moving them to assembly areas southwest of airfield 1. The marines in the vicinity were not pleased that the Shermans had settled there: the tanks were drawing artillery fire both from Suribachi behind us and from the hills around airfield 2 ahead.

I first set foot on the sands of Iwo Jima at about noon on 23 February, and I felt we had, indeed, as Prometheus had, reached the remotest region of the earth, a wilderness without a footprint. Any imprint was immediately filled and covered by the loose, ever-shifting volcanic soil. If you remained in one spot for any length of time, your ankles were grasped by the sand, and you sank deeper and deeper. When you laboriously moved on, tracks instantly covered themselves.

There is no grass, no real vegetation, only an occasional gnarled tree, twisted and bent into an abject position as if in punishment for having challenged the profound barrenness of Iwo. The recent extensive additions to the seascape only accentuate the desolation: misshapen hulks of wrecked ships, capsized AMTRACs and Higgins boats peppered with hastily discarded helmets and assorted combat gear, tanks destroyed by antitank guns and land mines, Japanese planes decimated while trying to escape attack.

I do not tarry on the beach. I am surrounded by a crescendo of whistling mortars, artillery shells, and whirring rockets, all followed by thundering blasts. Then the screams. A brief quiet before the ubiquitous cry, "Corpsman!" There are never enough corpsmen as they, too, fall victim to the onslaught. I have learned on Bougainville and Guam to recognize when the whistling is headed in my direction. I dive under a disabled tank or hug a revetment. If the interval between bursts shortens, I move on quickly. It means they have zeroed in on that spot. The whirring of the rockets is something new, and I don't take any chances.

I don't bother to brush off the dirt as I get up and move on among the mangled torsos, the scattered limbs, the most recently wounded, and the stretcher bearers bringing casualties from the brutal fighting up ahead to be ferried to the *Samaritan* or the *Solace*. Some of the young marines sit with haunting, vacant stares—the hollow men, rigid in the benumbed silence of combat fatigue. They don't bother to dive for cover. I touch a shoulder, open a canteen, help light a cigarette, but I don't linger. I want to get on with my job. It's easier that way.

As I move beyond the high terraces toward the airfield, the sounds change to those of rattling machine guns, grenades, our 105-mm and 155-mm howitzer blasts, and the horrendous, swishing roar of flamethrowers.

I join Spiller and Gindreaux at the bunkers. We are at the very southeastern tip of the airstrip. I shake my head and can hardly draw my breath as I turn and look back from this commanding view over the fields of fire that the former occupants had over our landing beaches. I climb on top of one of the bunkers and turn toward Motoyama airfield 1, where before me spreads an expanse of wasteland perforated by bomb craters and eerie geysers of sulfurous mist—an expanse broken by the silhouettes of derelict tanks and planes and bodies half-rising as they stiffen grotesquely. My recent unmediated encounter with the flux of things only serves to darken the vistas on this piece of volcanic rock.

Earlier this morning the 21st Marine Regiment relieved the 23d Marines under cover of darkness and now is continuing the attack. This kind of maneuver—four thousand men replacing the shattered remnant of another regimental combat team—is a delicate operation at best; under cover of darkness it can be chaotic. The Japanese are fully aware of the procedure and are exerting immense pressure on that sector, which was also the junction of the 4th and 5th Divisions. Henceforth this will become the center of the American drive. The men of 3d Division's 9th RCT are coming ashore at the same time that we are landing with our tanks and soon the assault will consist of three marine divisions abreast.

Today the 21st Marines are being hammered by withering enemy fire as they try to move forward from the northern embankments of airfield 1 to the higher plateau of airfield 2. From the fortified network of caves, tunnels, and bunkers, coordinated deadly rainstorms of knee-mortar and machine-gun fire are pouring on the fresh troops; the ravines between airfields 1 and 2 are becoming the killing zone of this phase of the battle for Iwo Jima.

Airfield 1 is now nominally our territory, but it is not really under our control. Across the thirty-five-hundred-yard front at this widest part of the island are dozens of bypassed pockets of resistance. Japanese snipers are rampant. Vehicles and troops using the airstrip for passage north are clear artillery targets from Hill 382, an elevation northeast of airfield 2 and, second to Suribachi, the highest point on the island.

The congestion on the beach increases as our tanks and fresh troops pour ashore. An agitated Capt. Julius Lemcke confronts me as I come down from the bunker. He has been with his two platoons on the front lines.

"Where's the major?" he asks.

"He's over at division CP [command post], hopefully getting some orders." I know Lemcke's problem. His company is split: part is attached to the 4th Tank Battalion, and the remainder, of course, have come ashore with me and Able Company. Having been a company commander, I understand his concerns. "Lemcke, Colonel Collins of the 5th Tank Battalion is in charge up there. We are on radio silence, and until we get orders, there's nothing we can do. Did you suffer any damage?"

He shakes his head. "But the 4th and 5th are getting the hell beat out of them. We used some of my tanks against caves and machine gun nests. Tomorrow they're going to need more, and I want my company together."

I am empathic but not helpful. "You know we can't do that without corps or division orders. Spiller and Gindreaux tell me that Joy and his tanks are in reserve in a defile at the end of this trip, over to the left. We are going up there now. Want to come?"

"Let's go! We can only get up there through the 24th Marines sector." He points east, to our right.

Capt. Julius Lemcke is a committed marine officer. He has made it his mission to know everything there is to know about tanks. His is a technical and mechanical expertise to which we all defer. He really wants to transfer to the Marine Air Wing—which he will, indeed, later do. He is very impatient in combat but has the complete confidence and devotion of his men. Lemcke feels that as long as he is here, he should be fighting. Above all, he wants his company together.

On Iwo, no one walks upright. We crouch, run, and crawl. At times, fleeting images of the evolutionary process running in reverse dart through my mind. Winding through the gullies and ravines, it takes us nearly an hour to traverse less than fifteen hundred yards of "our" territory. As we approach the tank bivouac area, we see four tanks firing 75-mms from airfield 2. In the ravine, on our left, I recognize some Baker Company tanks with units of the 21st Marines.

Lemcke's six tanks are near the pass leading to the strip. He starts for the pass as I head toward the forward observation outpost of the 5th Tank Battalion among the ruins of a Japanese pillbox overlooking the near end of the airstrip. Lt. Col. William Collins is talking on the SCR (signal corps radio) with some of his forward tanks. We all scramble as a mortar barrage hits the area. He keeps talking on the hand radio. After a few minutes, he beckons to me.

"It's been like this all day," he remarks. Yes, our tanks have been assigned to him. He has used some in support of the 21st Marines, who are really being battered. The tank flamethrowers and tank-mounted rocket launchers are the most effective weapons up here. He has used the 2d Platoon of Baker Company on a probe along the left runway, but the mortars are too much. No infantry can stay up there. Right now the tanks on the airfield are firing rockets at some bunkers on the hills to the east. He doesn't think this will make much difference. The emplacements were too well-built, even against the direct fire from the tanks.

"But, hell, it does keep the bastards from shooting at us," he reasons. "However, when we try to put more tanks up there, all hell breaks loose. It draws mortar and artillery on the infantry." At this point, Colonel Collins doesn't need more tanks from our Charlie Company. He will use what he has to protect the sector between the 21st Marines and the 4th Division. He wants Joy to be in support of his tanks on the airstrip tomorrow. "You will all be here soon enough," he predicts.

Lemcke accepts the logic of the situation, and I go over to Quentin Joy. We agree on his exact present location on the grid map (182) although Colonel Withers might want him to fall back to an area in 164 to set up machine-gun coverage for the 21st during the night.

"At any rate, we won't be far from here. We haven't moved fifty yards all day." Joy points up to airfield 2 ahead. "There are only two little passes that the bulldozer could clear for tank access. The Japs have them both covered with antitank guns. Collins has already lost four, maybe five, tanks getting up there." We recognize the whistle and both hit the deck as the mortars come in again.

"Corpsman! Corpsman!!" To our left two marines have been hit with shrapnel. One's helmet is badly dented, but the scalp wound is not deep. Joy yells for a first-aid kit to be brought from his tank. The other marine has a bad cut on his leg, and there's nothing much we can do until the corpsman gets there.

An infantryman from the 21st Marines yells down. "Can't you park those fuckin' tanks someplace else?" Joy shrugs his shoulders.

In about five minutes the corpsman arrives. Spiller and I start back.

In less than an hour we wind our way back to the command post's two bunkers. Communications equipment is in place. Each concrete blockhouse is about ten-by-twenty-feet, with a five-foot ceiling. The blockhouse on the left contains two field cots—Major Evans will use one of them, and Jerry Foster and I will use the second alternately during the night when the other of us is at work in the adjoining "operations bunker." They haven't wasted any precious water cleaning the blood-splattered surfaces inside these structures.

Major Evans is back with the news that tomorrow all of our tanks will revert to 3d Tank Battalion control. Gindreaux, Spiller, Bob Mann, and I plot the location of the companies and Lemcke's two platoons. Only one thing—to my later regret—do we neglect to establish: the exact location of the 21st Marine Regimental Combat Team's command post.

. . .

On 24 February, D plus 5, everything is fragmented. Baker Company and two platoons of Charlie Company are up front (grids 182 and 183) supporting the 21st Marines who are temporarily attached to the 4th Marine Division. Able Company, with Headquarters Company and the remainder of Charlie Company tanks, is poised to enter on the east-west runway of Motoyama airfield 1 (grid 164).

Lieutenants Spiller and Gindreaux, Sergeant Mann, and I retrace our paths of the day before to join Captain Joy in the 21st Marines sector. Lemcke has moved over to the right to support the 25th Marines. We know things are bad even before we arrive.

Beginning at about 0900, the battleship *Idaho* and the cruiser *Pensacola* shell the area beyond the front lines with an intensity and ferocity that was horrendous. I have never been this close to the impact area of fourteen-inch naval gunfire. It is unsettling beyond description, even for those it is intended to reassure. Our artillery barrages follow. There is once again the period of relative silence between the preparatory shelling and the assault.

As the tanks from the 4th and 5th Tank Battalions start through the passes, Japanese artillery, antitank guns, and mortars hit the area with stunning accuracy. This attack gratuitously underscores a reality that the V Amphibious Task Force has certainly accepted by now: General Kuribayashi's fortress of reinforced concrete emplacements, tunnels, underground communications, and ordnance inventoried over years would not be neutralized by the heaviest of armaments.

As the 21st Regiment starts its drive, the Japanese general unleashes all of his artillery and mortar firepower into the area around the tanks. From blockhouses, bunkers, maze upon maze of caves, and camouflaged tanks, enemy weapons shower fire on every avenue of approach. Soon Kuribayashi's troops, though temporarily dazed, charge into the areas separating the 3d, 4th, and 5th Divisions. Two of Colonel Collins's tanks are hit by anti-tank fire and are blocking the passes. The Baker Company bull-dozer goes to help. Charlie Company tanks are able to move ahead against enemy caves and emplacements in the ravines to the east and right of Motoyama airfield 3.

Colonel Duplantis and his 3d Battalion of the 21st RCT start their drive without the Shermans. The airstrip has to be taken. Horrified, we watch as the men of the 3d Battalion and their offi-cers suffer some of the greatest casualties of the campaign. Our bulldozer, after clearing an approach around one disabled tank, is itself hit by three mortar bursts. Its suspension system badly dam-aged, the vehicle careens wildly into a bomb crater. A squad of infantry braves the mortar and machine-gun fire to protect the crew as they abandon the smoking vehicle.

Finally the passes are opened, and the tanks are able to sup-port and protect the marines by spewing machine-gun fire at the Japanese soldiers and hurling 75-mm shells when emplacements are exposed. Tanks that can get to the sides of the airfield effec-tively neutralize pillboxes by using a combination of flamethrowers and machine-gun fire against the hapless, burning, fleeing enemy. Nevertheless, ten of our tanks are hit by antitank fire or mines. It is an especially chilling portent for us.

At about 1630 the marines begin falling back to a position that they can hold during the night, and I receive a message from Major Evans to meet him at our command post. He is with the division commander, Gen. Graves Erskine. I am sure we are to become, once again, the 3d Tank Battalion.

It is not quite dark when I return to the CP. Before entering, I climb on top of the bunker and concentrate on Motoyama airstrip 1, the only route we have to move all of our reserve Sher-mans up front. The bulldozers and Seabees have done a remarkable job of leveling the bomb craters and removing the mines on the north-south runway. I can see clearly the tracks of the vehicles that have made a roadway across there. The pass leading up to the runway, about fifty yards to my left, has been significantly widened since yesterday. A couple of jeeps and an amphibious truck returning from the front are racing toward me over the runway. To my left are four charred tank hulks and several crushed Japanese Zero bombers pushed aside.

Further up, I see marines digging foxholes on both sides of the roadway. That would be the 21st Marine area. I hear the whirrs! I scramble down and flatten against the concrete as the rockets fly over. It is the beginning of a harassment ritual by the Japanese that will continue throughout the night. Sometimes they hit an ammo or fuel dump; sometimes they hit a crowded evacuation station, adding second and third wounds to marines lying on the beach. These rockets are not very accurate, and many fall short. Last night, two landed next to our CP.

I go inside and join Major Evans, Captain Foster, and some staff. We have no specific orders for tomorrow, and anxiety is hanging heavy. Captain Joy and our Company B have been assigned to continue support for the 21st Marines for the night, but clearly that regiment cannot continue the assault. We hear and see the men of the 9th Regiment grouping all around us.

My ordeal begins with the ringing of the phone at about 2130. It's Colonel Withers. The sergeant major gives the line to Major Evans. The 9th Marines will pass through the 21st tonight. Using the cover of darkness, they will be in the front lines at 0500. They want to use two tank companies to lead the drive.

"Able Company is ready, Colonel," Evans assures him.
Pause.
"At midnight?" Holly looks at me.
Pause.

"He's here. At your CP? Now?" Major Evans puts his hand over the phone and addresses me. "He wants you over there tonight." He motions for me to pick up the other line. Colonel Withers is always direct. The 9th will pass through his regiment at 0400. They want all the tanks in position by 2400.

"What position, Colonel?" I inquire.

"In Joy's area."

"I know where that is. I was there today."

Colonel Withers continues. "The 9th's officers are here now. They want you here."

"Tonight?" I venture.

"Not 'tonight.' Now!"

"Colonel, where's your CP?"

"I'll send an officer to meet you. There are two tank shells about five hundred yards up the runway on your left. Just beyond that, there's a pillbox on the left side of the runway. He'll be there."

The image of the marines digging foxholes on the airstrip flashes through my mind. "Colonel, do your men know I'm coming through your lines?" I'm aware that perspiration is flowing down my face.

"They'll know you're coming. Know the password?"

"Yes, sir. Colonel, who's the officer I'm looking for?"

"Lieutenant Bertelli. Angelo Bertelli."

"Notre Dame? The All-American?" I realize it is a stupid question.

"Yeah. Bert, bring another man along. It's better if there are two of you."

I hand the phone back to the sergeant major. Jerry Foster hands me a canteen cup of coffee and a cigarette. I look at Jim Gindreaux. "What's the password tonight?"

"States." Then he grins. "I think."

"Jim," I say, "have Bill Stone and the platoon leaders here by the time I get back from Withers."

Major Evans is concerned. "Bert, take Sergeant Mann with you. Jim, tell Bob what it's about, and get him over here."

The sergeant major offers, "Captain, do you want one of the tommy guns from the headquarters tank?"

That's not for me. "Are you kidding? I'd kill more marines than Japs with one of those. Besides, it's not the enemy I'm worried about. It's trigger-happy friends."

Actually, I'm worried about mortars, artillery, rockets, and defensive lines of machine-gun crossfire as well as land mines on that part of Motoyama 1. My stomach is churning far beyond the nausea to which I have become accustomed.

I join Bob Mann outside the CP. I have a lot of confidence in Sergeant Mann. Though he's not much older than I, his premature gray hair and penetrating gray eyes give him an older appearance that is consistent with his proven resourcefulness. He has been a member of Oscar Salgo's reconnaissance platoon, which is attached to the division temporarily. We work well together, and I encouraged his transfer to our operations section. He is sensitive to the infantrymen around us in combat. "They don't have all that steel surrounding them. Don't get too far ahead," he constantly reminds us.

The nights on Iwo are not just chilly; they are cold. The jackets that we are issued barely suffice, but right now that doesn't matter. I am soaking with sweat as I climb on top of the bunker and motion Bob to follow me. He has a tommy gun slung on his shoulder. We crouch as low as possible and yet can still observe the airstrip when the parachuted star shells periodically burst and drift. We determine our route. The flares seem to be on a four- or five-minute cycle. During the next "light time" we locate the two tank hulks about three hundred yards along the side of the roadway. I don't see the pillbox. Mann thinks he does. I point successively to three bombshell craters between us and the tanks.

"We'll follow them. There are probably some marines in them, so keep giving the password. We'll take off as soon as the flares die down."

A couple of mortar or artillery bursts are fired over to our right in the 4th Division area. Marines from the 9th Regiment are moving around us and seem to be advancing along the route we have been using to get up to the front lines. We climb down and walk over to the pass, muttering "Georgia," "New Jersey," and mostly "Connecticut," which the Japanese will have some trouble imitating. As we enter the pass, one of the marines asks, "Where the hell are you going?"

Bob shakes his head. "I'm not sure."

I secure my map case and button the snap on my .45 holster. I don't want to lose my equipment while running and crawling around out there. Besides, I have no intention of shooting. In this situation, where or whom do I shoot? We bolt out of the pass, crouch, run, and shouting "Georgia," dive into the craters. There are no marines there, but from the foxholes there comes, "Who the hell are you?"

"Going to the 21st CP." No one seems to have been aware that we were coming, but they accept our reply calmly enough.

The star shells open again as we are preparing to leave the crater nearest the tanks. Mann points ahead to a concrete structure on the side of the runway about a hundred yards ahead. Then it all comes down! The mortars and artillery pour onto the 21st Marine area, including the runway around the tanks. The fragments are flying in every direction, and we scramble under one of the tanks. Metal is clanking off the steel Shermans. Wounded marines are crying from their foxholes. I remember Thanksgiving Day on Bougainville when I was caught in one of these mortar storms. This is worse. The barrage lasts longer than usual, and there is consternation in the 21st Regimental Sector. Everywhere are the screams of the wounded and the inevitable shouts, "Corpsman! Corpsman!!"

The shelling lifts, and I crawl from beneath the tank and run to a crater near the pillbox. Mann leaps in beside me. "Cap'n, there's someone in that tank!"

"What?"

"There's somebody in that tank! I could hear them breathe and move. There's no bottom hatch."

A wounded marine tanker? A Japanese sniper? We both look back toward the derelict Sherman. It is more ghostly than ever. Bob Mann seems poised to go back. I grab his arm and nod toward the concrete box. "Let's go, Bob. We've got a job."

We make sure that our shouts of "Georgia!" "New Jersey!" and "Connecticut!" precede us as we approach the concrete pillbox. Nobody bothers with countersigns.

"Yaffe?"

"Yeah."

"Colonel Withers sent us." It isn't Angelo Bertelli, but we don't bother to pursue the matter as we follow the two men to the regimental CP.

Colonel Withers is on the phone assessing casualties from the mortar and artillery barrages. He is concerned about Japanese counterattacks or the large infiltrations that usually follow shellings of this ferocity. None yet. Major Kunz, regimental operations officer of the 9th Marines, and Lt. Col. Robert Cushman, commander, 2d Battalion, 9th Marines, are standing around a large gridded map spread on a table in the middle of the bunker. Colonel Kenyon, commander, 9th RCT, has designated his 1st and 2d Battalions as assault units to take Motoyama 2. Colonel Cushman has been assigned the critical left zone, straight up the runway. Lt. Col. Carey Randall is already in position and will take his 1st Battalion to the east, over the hills and through the ravines, to protect the right flank and tie in with the 4th Division.

Colonel Cushman and I have worked together on many training exercises and fought together on Bougainville and Guam. With close-cropped hair and chiseled features, he is the consummate combat marine officer. He beckons me toward the obligatory coffee and a cigarette.

Colonel Withers joins us. "Did you have any trouble finding it?"

"I didn't have any trouble *finding* it, Colonel, but we had some trouble getting here," I responded.

Colonel Withers has very little patience for small talk and is not known for his sense of humor. "Yeah."

I nod toward Bob Mann. "Colonel, Bob thinks there may be someone in one of the disabled tanks out there."

Colonel Withers frowns. "They're not disabled; they're destroyed." He looks at Mann. "We'll check it out tomorrow. I want them off the strip anyway. I think the Japs are zeroing in on them as markers." He turns to me. "You shouldn't have been under there in the first place."

"I think you're right, Colonel," I affirm. Cushman and Kunz smile. Colonel Withers ignores it. He wants to get on with the briefing.

At 0730 there will be naval shelling: the marine pilots in Corsairs will strafe the hills around Motoyama Village with 50-caliber machine guns. Cushman's Battalion will pass through Colonel Duplantis's 3d Battalion, and he wants Able and Baker tank companies up front as he starts across the strip.

Colonel Cushman points to the map and sweeps his finger across grids 183 and 201, each of which is subdivided into twenty-five lettered squares. Then he draws an imaginary line through the "Charlie" and "Dog" blocks on each grid. "We are concerned with this ridge, Charlie-Dog Ridge, and the hills beyond. The 24th Marines did get to Charlie-Dog today, but we don't really know how secure they are. The Jap engineers have constructed and camouflaged the toughest big-gun emplacements in those hills that we've ever run into. Naval and air bombardments are not getting them. It's going to take men and tanks. A lot of tanks."

He points to the Village of Motoyama, north of the airfield, and moves his finger to an elevation marked "Hill Peter," northwest of the airstrip. "Charlie-Dog continues around the airstrip and, with these hills, forms an amphitheater. The runways are the stage. There'll be no protection for us except for your tanks." He almost whispers, "Hill Peter is where we're going."

Cushman sips his coffee and continues. "Our howitzers will start the preparatory barrages shortly after 0800. The problem is that when the tanks go up with the infantry, we move too slowly and their mortar fire is too deadly for us. I want you to get one company on each of the runways at 0930 and move as fast as you can to right here." He points to "X" in grid 200. "Destroy every target of opportunity that arises. There'll be plenty of those when my men start across the strip. Once they join you, we'll go back to tank-infantry tactics."

I instinctively turn to Colonel Withers, a former tank officer. "Colonel, those tanks are going to be sitting ducks for AT [antitank] guns from those hills." I point to Hill Peter and Hill 382.

He and Colonel Cushman speak, almost in unison. "There's no other way."

Colonel Withers turns to me. "Most of the AT fire we got today was from Charlie-Dog, and the 24th Marines are up there now." He points to the airstrip on the map. "We've been over part of this area today. Collins's machine guns detonated most of the horned mines. We don't know what's up ahead, other than a lot of fire power."

I nod. "I know. We were there with Joy."

Colonel Cushman tries to reassure us—and himself. "We'll have the 12th Marines artillery in direct support. If you can identify AT fire, they'll lay it on." He stops, shakes his head, and speaks to no one in particular. "We've got to take Motoyama 2 tomorrow. It's costing too much human flesh!"

I address Colonel Cushman. "Able Company is standing by. You know Captain Bill Stone."

Colonel Cushman nods. He points to a spot in the "Dog" block on the map. "I want him here as soon as possible."

I look at Colonel Withers. "You have some men in foxholes out on that strip. We'll be going through within the hour. Is that all right? When the tanks begin to move up, the mortars and artillery will come again."

"We know. The 21st will draw back to here." Colonel Withers points to the spot where we are presently gathered.

"What about Joy?" I ask.

Colonel Cushman interrupts. "We already have a company relieving Duplantis's men. Let Stone's company assemble around your Baker Company."

"It's awfully crowded in that area," I offer.

"Hell, we know that," Colonel Withers continues. "Once the drive starts tomorrow, the 21st and Company C tanks will follow and mop up whatever areas the 9th bypasses. Division has promised me men from a replacement pool that landed today."

Cushman wonders, "Where the hell do they come from?"

I say to Colonel Withers, "You have the only direct line to Joy. Can I speak to him? I want him to meet Stone and help them get into position."

The colonel nods to the communications sergeant over by the array of equipment. "Get Captain Joy from Baker Company."

I address Colonel Cushman. "Colonel, Stone will start out as soon as I get back. The lead tank from each platoon will have its lights on until they get through the passes at the north end of Motoyama 1."

He nods. "My men will contact him, and I'll give him directions before 0400. See you tomorrow at my CP right here." He points to a spot that's Colonel Duplantis's forward outpost, among some blockhouse ruins. "Make it about 0800. I don't want too many people up there before then."

It's now 2230. The session is over. I wait until Joy is on the line. I brief him, and he will be waiting for Bill Stone at the end of the airstrip. No, none of the crew of the bulldozer is hurt.

I ask Colonel Withers, "Is there another way back other than over that damn strip?"

He points to the area to the west and south of us. "Yaffe, the 5th Division has been fighting counterattacks and infiltrators for two nights. There are some worried marines out there. Password or no password, I'd go back the way I came." I'm sure I sighed as Bob Mann and I put down our canteen cups and stubbed out our cigarettes. Colonel Cushman smiled. "And, Yaffe, disabled or destroyed, I'd stay away from those damn things on the runway."

Other than being frightened by the enemy rockets flying overhead, we go back to the CP without incident. It is always faster going back. Holly Evans and Bill Stone are waiting. Again, the coffee, the cigarettes, and the briefing. Able Company is ready. Stone and his officers—Lts. Bill Day, Jim King, Clair Griffin, Bill Richardson, and Marty Walters are all present. I relay our orders very quickly. Major Evans adds that he and I will move up with headquarters and the remaining tanks from Charlie Company at dawn.

The briefing is—brief. Within five minutes, the Shermans' engines begin to roar, and tank commanders on foot guide the tanks to the two passes that lead to the airfield. Though we've seen it dozens of times, it is an awesome spectacle as these behemoths accelerate and, with weapons unsheathed, hurtle across the moonscape of Motoyama 1. There's a sudden staccato burst of machine-gun fire from the 21st Marines as two desperate Japanese snipers are cut down running from the derelict tanks.

At about 0100, Colonel Withers calls Holly to inform him that all the tanks are in place. And, yes, tell Yaffe that Sergeant Mann was correct—there were some Japanese in that tank.

The canteen cup in my hand won't stay still. Capt. Jerry Foster suggests that I try to get some sleep. Major Evans and I go into the other bunker, and I pour water from a five-gallon can into my helmet and try to clean up. Holly nods toward one of the cots. J. D. Kirkham has dropped off some fresh skivvies, dungarees, and extra blankets that he managed to get from the quartermaster's dump down on the beach.

"And, here." He hands me a green sweatshirt. "He also got a couple of these."

"How the hell does he do it?" I marvel. The sweatshirt feels warm against my quivering chest.

The Coleman lantern casts an eerie light on the flamethrower-charred and bloodstained concrete walls of the bunker. I lie on the cot and pull two blankets over my chilled, trembling body. My head is feverish. Maybe it's the malaria. I close my eyes and hope for some sleep. I don't recall having slept on Iwo or for the final days on the LST.

I can't breathe. Again, the crypt! The concrete closes in, and it's Bougainville again, only worse. I begin to gasp. I stand.

"What's the matter?" Holly asks.

"I can't catch my breath! I've got to go outside." I struggle into the fresh dungarees, throw a blanket around me, and go into the darkness just outside.

Holly follows me. "You all right?"

"I think so. I'll sit out here against the bunker."

He brings me my helmet and poncho. "Will coffee, a cigarette help?"

I retch. "I'll be all right. Get some sleep. I'll call you if I need help."

He tries to distract me and points down to the beaches, where mammoth boats are unloading under full lights. "You'd think we were on the docks at San Francisco. Amazing that they are not hit more than they are."

I try to acknowledge his helpfulness. I point to the volcano. "I think the Japanese on Suribachi have enough on their hands."

He leaves, and again I try to close my eyes. It gets worse. I can't breathe at all. I pant. I stand and pace in a small circle. To assuage the foreboding that has overcome me during the days immediately preceding this campaign, I have relied on thoughts of Erna and the prospect that after this, I will be rotated back to the States.

I have rarely dwelled on thoughts of my own death, fearful they would be self-fulfilling prophecies. If the thought has ever intruded, I have brushed it aside with a loving image of Erna, visualizing our life together and our future family. At the age of twenty-four, one has so much to become and so much to witness. Such solace began to fail me, however, the afternoon I first walked along the shores of Iwo.

Although I am taking in enough air to stay alive, it doesn't feel like it. Images of the past four days keep flashing through my mind: flaming kamikazes, burning tanks on Motoyama 2, seeing brave young faces obliterated in a hail of machine-gun fire, crossing the airstrip with the expectation of an exploding mine preceding each step, experiencing suffocation inside the bunker-turned-crypt. Remembering Bougainville, I keep repeating, "If I can just get through the next ten minutes, I'll be all right. Just a few minutes!" Nothing helps, but my gasping increases in intensity.

There are two points of departure that in my contemplative efforts I have always found evocative. One is Julian Huxley's dependable "mankind is evolution becoming aware of itself." The other is Spinoza's plaintive insistence on viewing reality under the aspect of eternity. On the surface these two thoughts appear to lead in radically different directions. Eternity is obviously timeless, boundless, and incomprehensible to humans. Evolution is dealing both with a tactile environment and with time—duration, something I can comprehend. Still, my intuition insists that Spinoza is pointing to something that I should try to grasp, however metaphorically.

Seeking to ease my gasping for even a few minutes, I try to see things "under the aspect of eternity." To the historian, ten, eight, even six thousand years becomes a reverentially long period, even for the development of civilizations. But to the naturalist studying the evolution of life on earth, ten thousand years is a mere blip on a linear graph of four billion years. A geologist examining the evidence of the earth's earliest moment would extend the time line to about five billion. An astrophysicist calculating the origin of the cosmos would triple that figure to about fifteen billion; subatomic building blocks of all matter have been dancing out there that long.

I try Henri Bergson's metaphor of looking at evolution through a motion-picture camera, and I reverse the process, play it backwards. I speed through ages, through civilizations, through Rome, Athens, Jerusalem, Phoenicia, Samaria. The pace accelerates as I follow the naturalist through the human and the proto-human, a myriad of creatures and life forms I can only dimly imagine. So much has happened: more than ninety-nine percent of all life forms that have existed are now extinct. . . . Again the speed increases, but now my perception is that I am merely floating through dancing, swirling particles and waves. These evanescent, spinning phantoms are the last to which I can even remotely relate as I hurtle into and through a primordial vortex of force and heat of magnitudes that are infinite.

It is here that the mind's eye carries me beyond thought and imagination into a mother sea of timeless, formless, undifferentiated flux, the creative potential of all that is. But really, of course, time is not reversible. I cannot stay here. I thrust back through the threshold, the beginning, and back from eternity to what I am able to imagine, matter coalescing around energy, mind coalescing around matter. The flux crystallizes into all the successor times, places, and things that have become galaxies, mountains, and eyes.

Compressing the history of the universe into a single year, I hesitate briefly at the point when earthly humans first arrived, about an hour ago; then forward to the emergence of Homo sapiens, about ten minutes ago. The sweep of all this would be overwhelming were it not for the unity of the whole thing. Indeed, it's the unity that makes it all so gripping.

Ten minutes? That's all I was asking for. My breathing is easier. I feel a hand on my shoulder. It must have been much longer.

It's Holly. "Let's go, Bert."

0800 Sunday, 25 February, D plus 6. Major Evans, Sgt. Robert Mann, and I have stationed our headquarters tanks in a ravine between Motoyamas 1 and 2. We report to Colonel Cushman at his CP. Lieutenant Spiller is with Captain Joy as Baker Company prepares for the 0930 charge through the passes on the right and onto the north-south runway. The tanks will turn right at the intersection of the two strips and, on the east-west runway, will head toward the formidable Hill 382. Jim Gindreaux checks in with Capt. Bill Stone, whose Able Company will charge through the left pass and, keeping on the north-south strip, will head toward Hill Peter and Motoyama Village. Spiller, Gindreaux, and Warrant Officer Kellerman are checking SCRs 8 and 10 communications links among the platoons and infantrymen. Capt. Julius Lemcke, pacing like a caged lion, keeps reminding me where Charlie Company, finally together, is now parked. He and I walk back to the rubble of a demolished pillbox between Able and Baker Companies.

Warrant Officers Newton and Dabbert are there with the tank recovery vehicle. They have been talking to some of the tank crews, and Newton, as usual, is upset. "These tank gunners never have enough training," he complains. "Especially those who joined us after Guam."

Dabbert, unsmiling, has his usual riposte. "Find the referee. Call time out."

Lemcke is not amused. "These men are ready."

Kellerman is checking the gear in the communications jeep. He signals that all is ready. I notice Joy climbing onto his tank. The crews have capriciously named the Shermans alliteratively with the designation of the company. His tank, which was previously mine, has "Butcher" in bold white letters on two sides and in the rear. Bill Stone is already standing in his turret, checking the intercom.

At 0815 the preparation begins. One never becomes inured to fourteen-inch naval gunfire, five-hundred-pound bombs from the air or to heavy artillery fire flying overhead. Today the explosions are deafening, and the ground shakes with such fury that, reflexively, we turn toward Suribachi. Perhaps the damned volcano is erupting. The terror is heightened by our remembrance of numerous instances of deaths by "friendly fire." In fact, it happened yesterday. Newton and I go back to Cushman's CP and join the artillery officer from the 12th Marines. We're hoping to pick up some muzzle flashes from the hills, which might reveal enemy artillery or antitank emplacements. But nothing.

At 0910, there is no interval of silence between artillery preparation and ground assault, the solemn interlude that I have come to identify with casting the die of combat. We want to start before the artillery fire lifts.

As Able Company's Shermans churn through the pass on the left and the lead tanks—"Ateball," "Agony," and "Angel"—charge straight for the intersection, another layer of the Japanese defensive might is unmasked. Angel and Agony are hit by antitank fire from the hills ahead, and the instant smoke means trouble for the crew. Ateball makes it to the intersection and is hit by direct artillery fire. Able Company tanks keep coming.

On the right, Lt. Charles Kirkham leads his 1st Platoon of Baker Company out of the other pass and, through a storm of mortar shells, turns onto the east-west runway. The Japanese unleash three-, six-, and eight-inch cannons that have been camouflaged on Hill 382. Kirkham's tanks scurry to the left of the runway and fire the 75-mms into the area of the flashes from the big guns. Two of the tanks are hit by antitank guns, another by cannon fire. The crippled tanks keep firing, and there are two massive explosions as the cannons and their ammunition are destroyed.

Lt. Tom Hughes with Baker's 2d Platoon has followed Kirkham closely, but as the Shermans spread out to cover the area to the right of the airstrip, Hughes's tank is hit by an AT shell, and the suspension system is demolished. Mortars immediately pour onto the immobile Sherman.

The tanks from both companies keep charging onto Motoyama 2. Two of Lieutenant Cunningham's 3d Platoon, Baker Company, vehicles are hit by antitank fire as they enter the runway; the pass is blocked. In spite of the mortar fire, the crews abandon the tanks and help the tank retriever push the disabled vehicles aside. Soon both companies are on Motoyama 2, and the guns of twenty-five tanks are blazing.

The 9th Marines pour swiftly onto the airfield and form fighting teams as they coalesce around the tanks. We are now, however, moving into the very heart of General Kuribayashi's bastion, and he is prepared. From every macabre, sulfurous crevice and jagged ledge an automatic weapon is unveiled; from ravines and gorges— considered neutralized—come knee mortars and grenades. Mounds of rubble become camouflaged tanks. From Hill Peter and Hill 382 fly large projectiles we have not yet experienced as direct fire. The

Japanese soldiers have abandoned their banzai charge tactics and are effectively firing from hidden emplacements.

The tanks continue firing 75-mms and rockets at the flashes in the hills and employing machine guns and flamethrowers as endangered infantrymen identify more immediate targets. Although we are on the relatively high ground, the terrain is open, and the casualties keep mounting. Colonel Randall's 1st Battalion is trying to close the gap on our right. The fighting on the entire front reaches a fury beyond anything we have ever experienced. It is an unrelieved segue of horror and heroism.

On the left of the east-west runway, Kirkham's tank continues to be buffeted by mortar fire. He is concerned about the possibility that his ammunition, which has been exposed by the antitank shell, will explode. When the 9th Marines protectively surround him, he orders three of his crew out. He and his gunner, Robert Schimmer, remain and continue to expend all of the ammunition on targets that are continuously revealing themselves.

On the other runway Cpl. Bill Adamson worms through the twisted turret and escapes from the smoldering Agony. On the ground, he is hit in the leg by machine-gun fire and crawls toward the crippled Ateball as it continues firing away. The crew see him and signal for him to remain where he is. They drop the bottom hatch, and like a protective though wounded elephant, the Sherman straddles the prone Adamson; the crew members then pull him into the crowded tank. He is able to identify for them the positions of two antitank weapons as well as the machine-gun nest that hit him. Ateball rapidly demolishes them all.

The violent storm of fire continues. The officers and men of the 9th Marines are suffering the same severe casualties that we witnessed yesterday among the 21st RCT. We don't know yet how many of our crewmen are killed or wounded. We do know that fifteen of the twenty-five tanks have taken direct fire or mine damage. Colonel Cushman gives me permission to directly coordinate the artillery fire with targets that our platoon leaders are identifying. We locate and—with the 12th Marines' howitzer fire—neutralize many of the enemy's heavy gun positions that are bearing down on the airfield. When I concentrate on the east-west runway, the names of the tanks melt away as I focus on the men inside, men I have trained with, fought beside, and lived with for years: Harry Trefsgar, Wallace Smith, Paul Engle, Tom Murphy, Frank Rawcliffe, Bob Jeter, Billy Cawdill, Everett Shrock, George Udseth, Jim Thornhill. . . .

Thornhill! His tank is able to get nearly a hundred yards beyond Kirkham's and is devastatingly effective—for a while, before being hit by artillery. The left side is badly damaged. The hulk rocks from side to side as the mortars keep pouring on. Smoke rises from every slit. The thought of Thornhill is particularly painful for me as it mingles with flashes of Erna—both so full of life. Thornhill, the youngest of the young.

In midafternoon Colonel Kenyon, commander of the 9th RCT, sends his 3d Battalion, under Lt. Col. Harold Boehm, to reinforce the 2d Battalion so that we can hold Motoyama 2 and prepare to push on tomorrow. Some of Cushman's men have reached Hill Peter, but not enough of them to hold a position. His battalion suffered losses of four hundred men, killed and wounded.

Later we are able to get to Kirkham and Schimmer and retrieve their tank. They are unharmed. Unfortunately we cannot reach Thornhill's tank before our infantry has to fall back as our artillery shells start to pour. Thornhill is killed, and the assistant driver, Roger Mello, is gravely wounded. As we begin the painful process of evacuating the wounded, removing the dead, and recovering vehicles that are salvageable, other tanks continue to attack pillboxes and gun emplacements, with infantry and demolition teams following closely. The 3d Tank Battalion has nine vehicles knocked out of action; seventeen crewmen are killed or wounded.

Despite all the frenzy in this very center of the front, as we prepare for the night, we have gained only a few hundred yards. We have a position, however tenuous, on Motoyama 2 and have relieved the pressure on Motoyama 1. There is now a steady flow of ammunition-carrying and supply vehicles on that strip. As darkness sets in, Warrant Officers Dabbert and Newton and Sergeants Sprint and Doggett have ordnance and maintenance crews repairing those Shermans not completely destroyed. And, of course, Captain Lemcke and Charlie Company are ready for tomorrow.

The two-day battle for Motoyama airfield 2 has been costly for all three tank battalions. With tanks being deployed against direct artillery and antitank fire in our effort to attain the high ground beyond the airfield, the battle has greatly depleted our tank corps.

Beginning on 26 February, Charlie Company is attached to Colonel Randall's 1st Battalion, 9th RCT, as he continues the push through the ravines and hills east of the airfield. We revert to the tank-infantry warfare that had proved most effective. The Shermans are used in units of platoons in direct support of infantry against limited, well-defined objectives—caves, bunkers, pillboxes, any strong pockets of resistance. Where possible, the tanks precede the infantry; where this is impractical, infantry leads, and we give direct-fire and flamethrower support. Day-by-day, yard-by-yard, the 9th and 21st RCTs leapfrog each other—with the 3d Tank Battalion always in support.

For me the days are mostly measured by sunrises, sunsets, midnight orders, H hours—and anguished witness. "Company strength," "tanks operative," "crews available," and "tanks recovered" echo in my head more and more insistently as we continue the march up through General Kuribayashi's ingenious honeycomb of bunkers, pillboxes, caves, and tanks buried in volcanic ash up to their gun turrets. This is the terrible terrain of killing grounds that we have come to know as the Meat Grinder.

Sleep comes to me, however briefly, during these nights—but not before I dissolve the stifling crypt around me and enter a realm of contemplative consciousness.

NINE *Ode to Joy*

22 March
3d Tank Bn (less Co. "A") embarked aboard LSTs 634
and 928 for Guam M.I.

Special Action Report, 3d Tank Battalion,
3d Marine Division, April 1945

There is no solution; seek it lovingly.

Variation on an old Talmudic saying

On the morning of 22 March 1945 the sun shone brightly, and some of the pall lifted from the death-haunted, craggy mass of volcanic rock that was Iwo Jima. I enjoyed a few hours on the top slab of the CP bunker, alternating calisthenics with writing to Erna and translating notes from my operations team's diaries into a report on the Iwo action. I went inside to gather up a sheaf of papers from the field table when Capt. Quentin Joy's tall, hunched frame appeared in the opening and he abruptly placed a brown bag in front of me.

"Happy birthday!"

I pulled out a bottle of Ballantine's Scotch whiskey. "Thanks. Where the hell did you get a brown bag?"

He hesitated, as he usually did before speaking. "You'd be surprised what we can get in the headquarters tank once we don't have to contend with your books and a chess set. We even found room for some ammunition."

"You all set to go?" I asked. Baker Company would be returning to Guam on LST 634. I would be going on LST 928.

"Yeah. We'll be shoving off about 1400. Jeter's getting them squared away. Thought I'd take a walk up Suribachi. I haven't been up there. The brochures all say it's the best attraction. Want to join me?"

I pointed to the papers on the table. "I want to give a draft of this action report to Holly to read aboard ship." I paused. "But what the hell? It's my birthday! A quarter of a century has passed, and there are two places I haven't visited—Yellowstone and Suribachi."

"This is a lot closer," Joy said as he picked up some yellow sheets of paper on which I had been writing. He started reading in exaggerated, mock officialese: "26 February. 0630—Company C attached to 1st Battalion, 9th Marines, for the day's attack. A platoon of tanks used in seizing the hill and high ground in vicinity of TA-200P. 0750—Company Command tank and one platoon report to Baker Company, 9th RCT. Attack coordinated with the infantry and the tanks moved around heavily fortified hill firing into caves and destroying pillboxes and bunkers. Flame-throwing tank used to burn out a cave from which enemy infantry were emerging on the base of the reverse side. The flamethrower exploded the ammunition in the cave. 0815—The track of one of the tanks was broken by an artillery shell believed to be a friendly short round. It was requested that our artillery barrage be lifted two hundred yards, which was done. The crew remained in the tank and continued firing at the enemy fortifications."

I was getting irritated, but Joy continued. "27 February. Baker Company attached to the 1st Battalion, 9th Marines; preceded their Love Company. 0730—Eleven tanks moved out in the advance. 0750—3d Platoon leader's tank was disabled by a mine. Three more tanks were disabled by mines in an attempt to maneuver around tanks that had been hit. During this brief action of approximately twenty minutes, six tanks were knocked out, and four men were killed. Ten men and three officers were wounded, and one man is missing in action. Excellent work was done by the tank crews in evacuating the wounded men."

He threw the papers on the desk. "I don't know, Yaffe. Tolstoy you ain't!"

I took offense. "C'mon, Quent. The nouns and verbs are all there. A few adjectives sprinkled around, and I think it'll compare very favorably to *War and Peace*."

He shook his head. After a pause he picked the papers up and, skipping about, continued reading rapidly. "1 March. 0630—All platoons of B Company report to 2nd Battalion, 21st RCT. 1102—Enemy tanks, used as emplacements, were spotted and destroyed. 1355—The 3d Platoon leader's tank hit by AT. After the crew evacuated, the enemy attempted to blow up the tank with dynamite. They were cut down by machine gun fire. 1510— Six tanks were employed in this action. Three of them were knocked out by enemy fire and remained on the front lines. During the night, two of these tanks were burned by the enemy. As a result of this action, eight of the enemy's tanks were destroyed and one truck, and numerous pillboxes and emplacements. One officer and three of our men were wounded."

I stood up and started gathering the papers. "Let's go, Joy." I wrote my name on the brown bag and put everything in a footlocker in a corner. I grabbed my shoulder pack. "Let's stop by the galley. I want to pick up some rations."

Motoyama 1 was a busy scene. Two Superfortresses had crash-landed yesterday, and Black Widow night fighters were now filling up the runways. We walked around the taxi strip to the area containing our tank-maintenance platoon and galley facilities. The men were breaking camp, but a young cook, "Paisan," retrieved a couple of C rations for me. Joy was thoughtfully gazing to our right, at the 3d Division cemetery. The body bags kept coming, and the white crosses were multiplying. His normally handsome features, below a head of thick black hair, were wrinkled into a scowl. I joined him and broke his reverie. "Let's go."

Quentin was a close friend. Over the past two and a half years, only I among all the officers had come to know him well. He was not an easy person to know, but he was a genuinely brave and humane man. His courage was unstudied, his humanity, instinctive. That day, I could tell, he was feeling a lot of pain.

When Capt. Len Reid, my predecessor as commander of Baker Company, returned to the States, I had appointed Quentin Joy to succeed me as company executive officer. He moved into the field tent that Len and I shared. Quentin had the annoying habit of excessively deliberating and delaying his response to almost any question, regardless of its significance or insignificance. In any conversation that involved more than two of us, it was as though there were several dialogues going on at one time.

There would be this period of inordinate hesitation and the discussion of several additional topics before Quent would reply to a previous question or respond to an earlier observation. It was so disconcerting to most of the officers that at mess many ignored him or wondered if he was all there.

Actually, Quentin Joy was brilliant; it was just that he took everything so seriously that it seemed he believed his every statement was a revelation of his inner self. He had little patience for people who spoke gratuitously. He didn't really care what others thought of him.

At each promotion that I gave to Lieutenant Joy, I had to convince Major Evans and Colonel Withers that he wasn't indecisive, just very deliberate. I knew his personal fortitude from our combat experiences on Bougainville and Guam, and my respect for him was widely shared among the men who fought beside him. Under fire, he was so intent that his annoying characteristics only accentuated his firmness and calm resolve. He was, as they say, a good man to have with you.

My enduring image of Quentin Joy is from that horrifying day on Motoyama 2. As the 9th Marines charges on the airstrip and join his besieged company, Joy flings open the turret hatch of his headquarters tank, takes the SCR hand radio from a fallen infantry reconnaissance man and directs the tank and infantry teams to attack the machine-gun pits on the hills and ravines immediately to his left. He is also trying to lead them to both Kirkham's tank and—much farther up—the smoldering Sherman that contained Thornhill and Mello. We stare incredulously when the hatch lifts, as though someone is trying to emerge. Japanese machine guns and knee-mortar shells immediately zero in on the turret, and the hatch snaps shut. The smoke and blaze intensify, and mortars continue rocking the tanks. The 9th Marines are caught in a deadly crossfire that we know is coming from areas we can reach neither with direct tank fire nor with flamethrowers. It is at this point that Major Evans and I ask for the artillery fire.

We clear the communications channels as I twice give the order for tanks to fall back to the intersection of the two airstrips. Colonel Cushman has already passed that command to the infantrymen, and with the exception of a squad that is with Joy, they are all retreating. I repeat the order to make sure that Joy hears it. He has flung his combat helmet off so that he can get the hand radio closer to his ear. He acknowledges the order but keeps pointing to the two disabled tanks. So I resort to the unambiguous language of marines: "Goddammit, Joy, this is an order! Get your ass back in that fuckin' tank, or I'll have you court-martialed! Now!" While the infantrymen rejoin their platoon, Quentin reluctantly picks up his helmet and slowly climbs aboard his tank, 155-mm howitzer shells raining down on the hills and ravines around him.

Quentin was from Iowa and was once an intercollegiate wrestling champion. Among other things, we shared an enthusiasm for bodybuilding. We acquired some twenty-pound weights, which the puzzled maintenance crew lugged around the Pacific in tool boxes. And once we established some semblance of permanent quarters—in New Zealand, on Guadalcanal, and on Guam—he and I would stake out routes to run daily. There was, of course, one understandable exception—the jungles of Bougainville.

Although an avid reader, Joy did not share my enthusiasm for philosophy; he had an abiding interest in history. We passed back and forth a tattered copy of H. G. Wells's *Outline of History*, always adding pencil markings in different colors and underscoring passages. I was seeking patterns; he looked for facts. The one volume of mine that consumed him was a book of Plutarch's essays—he started memorizing it when the pages began to disintegrate from the humidity of Bougainville.

When I moved to battalion headquarters in the dual role of battalion executive and operations officer, we did not see each other as often as before. It was a period during which, no doubt, I was not very affable. Nevertheless, I was sensitive to Joy's status as a loner and made it a point to find time for our periodic discussions about the world. They usually began with one or the other of us posing a fragment of thought, which would launch us into discussions conducted with a superabundance of youthful seriousness.

As we approach Suribachi today, I point to the summit. "They would have chained Prometheus up there," I say.

But Joy is preoccupied with his men: Harry Trefsgar and Wallace Smith. He describes in detail their deaths when the tank was immobilized by a mine and destroyed by AT fire. He has to reexperience pulling the bodies of Cpls. Thomas Yannotta and Willmar Woods from their flamethrower tank that became an incinerator. His anguish continues with vivid descriptions of Sgt. John O'Hara and Cpl. Mervin Birtcil, and then there are Jim Thornhill and Roger Mello. We couldn't get to their tank. Thornhill was dead, but Mello—gravely wounded—could not be reached until the next day by Pharmacist Mate Bill Dobbins, who risked his own life to evacuate him. "Imagine being in there all night," he sighs.

After a while he remarks, "They're so fuckin' young."

I nod.

He continues, "Some of them are not even twenty years old."

"I know how old they are, Quent," I muse. "We're all young."

When we reach the base of the volcano, we have a choice of three routes. The Seabees have created a superhighway over the original winding road, and the traffic is heavy with jeeps and four-by-four trucks. There is a steeper, less winding path that the infantry use. We can go straight up over the terraces, so we proceed to do that. We don't get far before my breathing becomes labored, however, so I head over to the infantry trail.

Joy follows. "What's the matter with you? We were running five miles on Guam."

I shake my head. "I wasn't smoking three packs of cigarettes a day then either."

The paths converge at about fifty feet from the summit of the volcano. There are a lot of communication and air force personnel working on radar installations all around, and two marine MPs (military police) at the junction. One of them addresses me as we start up the crest. "Captain, I wouldn't go any further. There are still some Japs with knee mortars and grenades in there." He points over to a squad of marines sorting some demolitions on a terrace over to our left. "They're going to send some explosives down."

I veer off to the left. "Thanks. This is close enough for me. I'm leaving today, and I'm not taking any chances." I go and sit on a hummock above the demolition squad. Joy is staring at the top of Suribachi.

He finally comes over shaking his head. "Can you imagine! The bastards are still alive. It's got to be over 130 degrees down there."

We sit quietly on the knoll for a while, contemplating this commanding position over the hapless landing beaches. Silence never bothers Joy or me. Eventually he looks around and asks, "Where would he have been?"

I couldn't fathom the question. "What the hell are you talking about?"

"Prometheus. You say they probably would have chained him up here. Where?"

"Joy, I said that an hour ago." I look around. After a while I point to a pile of rubble, the remains of a gun emplacement near the summit. "There! A perfect view of the 'flowering splendor of all-fashioning fire.' He was bound to that jagged rock. He saw it all." I think about that. Then I point to the crowded beaches and add, "But it was too much. It was too bloody even for the savage gods. They probably unchained him."

"Bullshit!" His vehemence attracts the marines. He lowers his voice. "If the horrors of war were a deterrent, there would never have been a war after Gettysburg."

I can't argue with him there.

Quentin laughs. "You know, Yaffe, you never tell that fuckin' Prometheus story the same way twice."

"It's not just a story; it's a myth. It's simple enough. In the beginning there were wars among the Olympian gods and the Titans. Prometheus, a Titan, sided with Zeus, the Olympian who emerged as the all-powerful god. The problem was not that absolute power corrupts. The problem was—and is—that absolute power is boring. Zeus wanted more playthings, a new race of creatures—human beings. He gave the task of creating these beings to Prometheus, who had proved to be so loyal in Zeus's ascendancy.

"Prometheus was a clever one. He did his job well enough, considering that Zeus forbid these creatures to have fire. He didn't want them warmed against the chill of reality. That humans endured at all is a tribute to the craftsmanship of Prometheus. He knew all about elementary particles and forces. But he had a flaw—compassion. He stole a torch from the eternal flame on Olympus and gave it to humans. Into the grim, frigid darkness he brought fire."

Quentin shakes his head. "From what we know about fire, I'd say 'compassion' is a dubious description. How did he presume to know what was good for mankind? Personally, Bert, I think your friend was an arrogant bastard." He laughs. "Of cosmic proportions."

I nod. "Zeus agreed. And he wasn't lacking in imagination when it came to punishing a rebel. He chained the firebringer to a forsaken summit and drove a spike through his stomach. There, he was at the mercy of an eagle who gorged on his liver all day long. But being a Titan, Prometheus couldn't die. Every night his liver grew back again. His torture was unceasing, but he never wavered in his defiance."

Joy interrupts. "Before, you always stressed that Prometheus was a seer, that he knew things that even Zeus didn't know."

"So?"

Uncharacteristically, Joy pounces. "Well . . . when he helped Zeus in war against his own brothers, Prometheus knew Zeus was going to win. Right?"

"Probably."

"Absolutely! And when he stole the torch, he knew what was going to happen to him."

"More than likely."

"*Much* more than likely. Prometheus didn't have a record of siding with losers." Joy pauses. "What the hell did he see in mankind that Zeus didn't see?"

"It's only a myth."

"It's a yarn," he insists.

I laugh. "My father would have said *bubbe meises.*"

"What the hell is that?"

I repeat slowly. "*Bub-eh my-seh*. It's Yiddish for 'old wives' tale.'"

"Exactly. Your father recognized a yarn when he heard one. He should have taught you better."

We both look out over the sulfur geysers to the landing beaches. By and by, Joy breaks the silence and points to the twisted twig of a pandanus pine trying to root in the volcanic ash. "Poor bastard. Doesn't have a chance."

Another silence. Then he blurts, "I don't agree with you, Yaffe. I don't feel any striving force in me. And we both know there's no grand design working here. I think the whole shebang was just a fuckin' accident, a crapshoot. A couple of atoms screwed around and made a molecule and, given enough time, here we are!" He hesitates, then points down to the white crosses and stars marking the graves below. "And there they are!"

What can I say? "It's all so fuckin' fragile."

There is spiraling smoke and sounds of tremendous explosions coming from the northern tip of the island. We both shudder. Bill Stone and Able Company are there with Colonel Boehm and the 3d Battalion, 9th Marines.

The silence again. Then, "Bert, what the hell can I write those families? I don't want to describe all that." He points to the airfields below. "What do I write? A lot of words about heroes?"

"I don't know, Quentin. You'll do it. Len Reid did it after Bougainville. I did it after Guam. You'll do it here. You'll do it. The words are important. It's all we've got."

"The words are important?" He shakes his head at the futility of the conversation. Then, to ease my frustration, he adds, "Accident, design, or striving force, I'll grant you this: after billions of years of blood, shit, and corruption, to have arrived at consciousness is a remarkable thing."

"Awesome!" I like this mood better.

He rises, saying, "I've got to be going."

I reach for my rations. "I'll stay here for a while. I don't think I'll be eating much when that LST starts to pitch and roll."

Joy dusts himself off. "And you're right, words are important. The question that you keep talking about—the meaning of life—is important." He pauses. "My problem with philosophies—with philosophers—is they see that question as a challenge like an ocean voyage, or a military campaign, something to be done with a particular goal in view, something to be formulated and fixed in place. And when it's formulated, to be ranted and pontificated from a pulpit. They are wrong. Plutarch said it clearly: 'Philosophy is not a chore to be got over with. It is a way of life. All your life, all your time, in everything you do, whatever you're doing, is the time for philosophy.' And so it is of that question." He starts down across the terraces. "See you back on Guam."

I open a C ration. "See ya."

As I watch him lumbering down the side of Suribachi, a thought strikes me. I look back toward the pile of rubble at the summit. I chuckle, and it becomes a guffaw. Then the laughter becomes uncontrollable, the guffaws louder. The demolition team looks up quizzically. I point to Joy descending and cry, "He's unbound!"

TEN *Fragility*

Not comprehending, they hear like the deaf. The saying is their witness: absent while present.

Heraclitus, *Fragments*

As my fit of laughter subsides, one of the marines from the demolition squad yells, "You all right, Captain?"

"I'm fine, thanks. How long before you're going to send those charges down?"

"We're almost ready. Waiting for a Jap language officer from corps headquarters. They want to try and get them to surrender."

I think of the conversation between Joy and me. "I hope they know the right words."

Another marine joins in. "I don't think the right words are in these Nips' vocabulary."

I finish the rations, shed my dungaree top, and lean back on my helmet as I bask in the rare Iwo Jima sunshine. I have some time, and something is gnawing at me. Like most of the others, I am functioning by reflex. I'm frustrated about leaving this place without having borne meaningful witness to the carnage of the past month. Have I been "absent while present"—precisely contrary to the role that contemplation had lead me to accept as my responsibility to life?

My foreboding about the real possibility of death lifted about two weeks ago with the realization that I would probably leave Iwo alive. These contradictory presentiments—the probability of my going home and the real possibility of my death—were intensified by an event on 8 March that still haunts my memory.

Our hold on airfield 2, however fragile, ends the initial phase of the Battle for Iwo Jima. The second phase—the grueling and gruesome advance through the Meat Grinder—begins the next day, Monday, 26 February, D plus 7. The bloody gorge is a labyrinth ingeniously designed to protect Hill 382, a bastion of artillery, rocket launchers, antitank guns, and 320-mm mortars. There is also a ring of hills—Peter, 362A, 362B, and 362C—ominously guarding the area. The ravines between Motoyama 2 and Hill 382 are the Valley of Death.

With the two regiments (9th and 21st Marines) of the 3d Marine Division in the center, the 4th Division on the right flank, and the 5th on the left, the American assault is measured in yards through the rugged terrain. The tank-infantry teams, always under heavy artillery and mortar fire from Hill 382, fight through the maze, pillbox by pillbox, cave by cave toward Hill Peter and Hill 362A. While tanks, bazookas, and flamethrowers are the most effective weapons, the marine infantryman with his rifle and grenades, as always, is the mainstay of the drive. Our tremendous naval and artillery barrages are only marginally effective and sometimes inflict casualties among our own marines, a fact adding to our anxiety.

The progress is uneven across the front, leaving numerous enemy strong points to fire on our units from the flanks. High casualties among commanders, platoon leaders, and seasoned noncommissioned officers rapidly deplete the leadership corps, and the body of troops in the field is becoming younger and less experienced. This heightens the poignancy of it all—the young marines' perseverance and bravery as they fight their way toward death.

The Japanese resistance remains so impenetrable that General Erskine, division commander, orders tactics that we have never employed before. The battalions attack the main objectives diagonally, which does succeed in out-flanking the Japanese but at a severe price in casualties. We expose all of our units to powerful bypassed pockets of Japanese fire power, the most notorious known as Cushman's Pocket.

We try to rotate our three tank companies in support of the two 3d Marine Division regiments. Charlie Company, under Captain Lemcke, is first in line, not having been directly involved on Motoyama 2. Our maintenance crews and recovery vehicles—always under heavy enemy fire—cannibalize disabled tanks so that we can regroup and relieve Charlie Company when necessary. It becomes clear that this will be sooner rather than later. By the end of the second day of phase two, another eleven tanks are severely damaged by mines, antitank fire, or direct artillery shells.

Members of the operations team—Lieutenant Spiller, Lieutenant Gendreaux, Sergeant Mann, and I—are the liaison between the tank companies and the marine regimental companies. We work with the maintenance and ordnance crews to salvage disabled Shermans for yet another thrust at caves and bunkers in the fortress network. Soon the organizational lines between companies and platoons become indistinct as we shift units from one parent organization to another, according to the dictates of availability. These days of unrelenting devastation become a blur. All except 7 March.

Northeast of the remains of Motoyama Village, in front of the commanding cliffs of Hill 362C, is the impregnable Cushman's Pocket. Japanese soldiers—troops of the crack 26th Imperial Tank Regiment—have skillfully utilized every inch of the formidable terrain by erecting pillboxes, building emplacements for antitank guns, and camouflaging tanks. Cushman's Pocket is the most perfectly devised fortification on the island and cannot be taken by frontal assault. Another strategy will have to be employed.

Tactically, throughout the war, marines have not launched attacks in the dark: at night, Japanese have counterattacked, and marines have remained on the defensive. Late in the day of 6 March, after a day of futile, deadly frontal assaults, however, General Erskine decides to change the rules: the decision is made for a predawn attack on Hill 362C in order to surround and outflank Cushman's Pocket. Sunrise will come sometime after 0630. The attack by units of the 9th Marines that are attached to the 21st Regiment will begin at 0500. The 1st and 2d Battalions of the 9th Marines will join the assault at 0715.

For the predawn attack there will be no artillery barrage, and we will reduce the succession of flares that usually illuminate the area in front of our positions. Most of the usual awesome American firepower will be muzzled because no one really knows how far our troops can advance and how soon they will be intertwined with the enemy. During the night a cold rain begins.

To avoid any preattack movement, we keep units of tank companies Baker and Charlie on front lines throughout the night. It is not an unusual decision, although it invites mortar and artillery barrages as well as occasional forays of suicidal Japanese soldiers with satchel charges of explosives. We bring ammunition and refuel under cover of darkness. We also rotate some of the crewmen who have been in action all day. The tanks will be ready to move out at 0715 without the noisy positioning that usually alerts enemy antitank guns. The signal for the attack will be a concentration of white phosphorous shells placed on Hill 362 to both envelop the enemy and mark our objective to distinguish it from Hill 331 some two hundred yards closer.

For the tankers, 0500 is the beginning of an eerie battle. All is in readiness but under complete radio silence. Those crews on the front line are prepared for counterattacks should the night maneuvers be discovered. The marines move out. It is a silent movie with none of the deafening preparations that usually precede us. Major Evans and I are in the two headquarters tanks about a hundred yards behind the front lines. We will move up later, when the main body of the 1st and 2d Battalions of the 9th Marines move out after a ten-minute artillery assault on Hills 331 and 362. But for now, I can hear no sounds other than the cold rain dropping on the metal and the heavy breathing of the crewmen around me.

I subdue my feelings of claustrophobia by the combination of meditation and emotional detachment that has become a survival technique for me in such circumstances. Continually witnessing the mangled bodies of comrades and enemies has calcified the sensibilities of us all. Often we respond to the most horrific and ghastly events with inappropriate humor or a shrug of the shoulders.

For tank battalion commander Holly Evans and me, all of this is compounded by the responsibilities of assigning units for each assault. The company commanders and platoon leaders are unflinching in the execution of each day's orders. Holly and I have learned to give the assignments unhesitatingly, no matter how much we agonize with one another. The officers appreciate the decisiveness, but their understanding does not lessen our anguish.

Today, Captain Joy and his Baker Company are supporting the advance echelon of the 21st Regiment and the 3d Battalion, 9th Marines, who are at this moment moving out. The tanks, however, cannot move until daybreak. Captain Lemcke and Charlie Company will support the main body of the 9th Regiment when they begin to move at H hour. The 4th Marine Division on our right and the 5th on our left will try to keep abreast of the center movement.

The interminable first half hour passes with only sporadic rifle fire and the occasional exploding of grenades. All the tank hatches are open. We hear random outbursts of shouts from the Japanese, followed by the firing of automatic weapons. About two hundred yards ahead of the front line, we can see and hear swishing flamethrowers cutting through the darkness. The surprise seems to be working.

The foul weather does not keep the sun from rising shortly after 0600. The marines are surrounding the foothills of Hill 362C, and the fighting suddenly explodes into a full engagement as the surprised enemy realizes what is happening. Baker Company tanks move out to support the now-beleaguered marines. According to plan, Holly Evans moves his headquarters tank up to the position vacated by Captain Joy's tanks. I will wait and follow Charlie Company on the right.

The artillery barrage begins at 0705, and after ten minutes of heavy firing from all sectors, we advance—but not far. General Kuribayashi's network of tunnels and caves is weakened but not crushed. The general settles for surrounding the advance troops of the Americans and concentrates his fire power on what he knows to be the main assault.

Japanese antitank weapons focus on Charlie Company as it moves in support of the main body of the 9th Marines. The fighting is fierce. My tank is blocked by two of Lemcke's immobilized Shermans. I leave the tank and, with the evacuated crews of the two disabled tanks, work my way to Colonel Cushman's command post. He is frantically trying to coordinate artillery fire so it will not imperil the remnants of two of his companies that have been cut off from the main force and are surrounded by the enemy in Cushman's Pocket.

In addition to Japanese mortars, sniper fire continues from every direction. I report to a lieutenant and move on to a ledge on a ridge that offers some protection. I keep the crewmen nearby in case they will be needed to replace wounded tankers. Through field glasses, I spot some Baker Company tanks in the rugged terrain at the base of Hill 362C. I scan the ground ahead and now can see clearly the cost in human flesh as the bodies of marines and enemy troops intensify the grotesquerie of the volcanic landscape.

A heavy-duty flamethrower from one of the tanks unleashes a stream of fire into a cave. The most horrifying scene in all combat inevitably follows as burning Japanese soldiers bolt forward, only to be cut down by tank machine guns. The flame has also reached a cache of enemy ammunition. The largest explosion of the battle erupts as a side of the hill belches forth ordnance and more bodies. To the men of Colonel Cushman's battalion immediately in front of me, this event is merely a momentary diversion. The lieutenant from Cushman's staff motions for me to join them at the command post, a saddle in the rocky ridges below.

The colonel wants a platoon of tanks to maneuver into the crags and craters where the remnant of his F Company, under Lt. Wilcie O'Bannon, is trapped. G Company will cover us if the tanks hit mines. These marines have been caught for hours in a vise of crossfire from half-buried Japanese tanks and well-camouflaged bunkers.

The company is decimated, and O'Bannon wants to salvage the half-dozen or so men in the shallow foxholes around him.

As I prepare to relay the orders to Lemcke, I mention to the colonel an incident that Sgt. Tom Murphy described yesterday: his tank and another dropped their escape hatches and rescued two wounded litter bearers by pulling them up into the tanks.

"I don't give a damn *how* you get my men. Just get them!" Cushman barks.

Once Lemcke has the order to send the tanks in, he doesn't wait for detailed instructions. Within minutes, three of the tanks charge into the saddle, firing machine guns and flamethrowers at the enemy—who are amazed at the tanks careening through, over, and around terrain so forbidding that the Japanese had not even bothered to mine it.

Predictably the Shermans draw horrendous mortar barrages. The gunners continue firing as tank commanders and drivers maneuver to O'Bannon's men. Over the radio I recognize the voice of tanker Roger Radabaugh as he establishes contact with O'Bannon. The behemoths drop their bottom escape hatches and, with uncharacteristic gentleness, roll over the foxholes as hands reach down and pull marines up into the laps of the crewmen. Completing the rescue mission, the tanks lumber back over the perilous ridges.

By nightfall Colonel Boehm's 3d Battalion has captured Hill 362C, and Company C has lost five more tanks. An antitank shell has hit one of the Shermans directly, killing two and wounding three of the crewmen.

Early on the morning of 8 March, our command post is busy. Able Company has two platoons attached to the 21st Regimental Combat Team, who are clearing caves and pillboxes along the beaches. All other units on the island are regrouping to continue the advance tomorrow.

We have broken the walls and connected the two bunkers. Capt. Gerald Foster, battalion executive officer, is in one area assessing personnel status while, in another, Lou Spiller and I are checking the available tanks. Holly Evans is at division headquarters. Company commanders and platoon leaders stream in and out with status reports, seeking orders.

Capt. Julius Lemcke charges in with his usual query: "Where's Major Evans?"

"At headquarters," Foster replies. "He won't be back for a while."

"I understand I have to get permission from the infantry battalion commanders to get to the tanks that were hit yesterday. We want to get the personal effects of the men who were killed." Lemcke looks at me.

Foster, a recent arrival, is not used to Lemcke's impatience, which sometimes borders on petulance. "You'll have to wait for the major," Foster insists.

Lou Spiller addresses Lemcke. "Cap'n, I was there late yesterday afternoon. That tank is pretty well burned."

Lemcke asks me, "Who's area is that in now? 9th or 21st?"

Foster interrupts. "Lemcke, nothing is going to change in the next few hours. I'll let you know when the major returns."

Lemcke ignores him and comes over to look at the situation map spread out on the table before me. I fold it up, put it in my map case, and walk over to get my helmet. "Jerry, I've got to check with Cushman and Boehm about tomorrow. Lemcke can come with me," I turn to Lemcke, "if he wants to."

As I leave the bunker and start through the pass, Lemcke catches up with me. We walk without speaking for a while. I feel surprisingly relaxed this morning. I slept soundly last night for about nine hours, exhausted from the past two days. More importantly, for the first time since landing on Iwo, I have a presentiment that I shall soon be leaving here, and I notice an ebbing of my emotional numbness. Lemcke, however, is on another train of thought. Five men in his company have just been killed or wounded.

Finally I break the silence. "Julie, you can be a pain in the ass."

"Yeah, I know. How else could I get to be an officer?"

We are approaching a cadre of replacements who are moving up to join either the 9th or the 21st Regiments. "They seem awfully young," I observe.

"They just look that way because they're clean and freshly shaven. Just off one of those LSTs," he murmurs.

"Lemcke, you know there's nothing in that tank worth risking a life for. What are you going to retrieve? A few letters? What personal effects?"

He shakes his head impatiently. "You were a company CO [commanding officer]. You know I'm not doing it for them. Bert, none of us ever imagined anything like this. We're all scared as hell, and about the only thing we can offer each other is the assurance that we care what happens."

I nod in agreement. "But getting hit by a sniper or a mortar shell won't help much."

We approach the corrugated terrain around Cushman's Pocket. Soon the trail will split: one branch goes down to our right and through to the area where the tanks were hit yesterday; the other leads up steeply to the battalions' command posts. As we get to the split, there's another platoon of replacements forming single file before going down into the pocket. At the head of the file, the young corporal who seems to be in charge warns, "Careful, Captain. There're a lot of snipers straight ahead."

I look at the ridges before us and reply, "Thanks. We're going up here to the battalion command post."

As I start the climb, a young marine squatting next to the point man stands up. "Got a smoke, Captain?"

Always the eyes! No older than Thornhill—he must have lied about his age, too. The eyes are blue. The words asking for a cigarette, the eyes asking for some reassurance. I can only give the cigarette, but I force myself to try for more. "Where are you from, Marine?"

"Texas, sir." He smiles, happy for the connection.

I nod. "Keep the pack. I've got more."

"Thank you, sir."

Lemcke is looking down toward the tank hulks. "You coming?" I ask as I continue up the trail to the left.

Colonel Cushman ignores Lemcke's question and addresses me. "Are there any things in or on those tanks that you need for replacement?"

I shake my head. "No, sir. We pretty well stripped 'em yesterday. And the bodies have been removed."

Two sniper shots, maybe three, come from the pocket to our right. The colonel is momentarily distracted, then ends the conversation. "I'm not risking another man for that. We don't really know how much damage we did down there yesterday. We're sending a company down and, if we can take some ground, you can check with me tomorrow." Nodding toward a group of officers having coffee near a bunker, he tells me, "Join them. I'll be over there shortly, and we'll talk about tomorrow."

Lemcke and I lock eyes. He exaggerates a salute, turns abruptly, and strides back down the path.

Cushman shakes his head. "Is he nuts? The last thing I need is a salute in sniper territory."

I laugh lamely. "I think he was saluting me, Colonel." I join the other officers.

Soon Colonel Cushman joins his staff and me and announces he has just received orders that the 21st Regiment, not the 9th, will take the offensive from here. His men will have another day to rest and regroup. I head back to the tank area to await orders from the 21st Marines.

As I walk down the steep path, I am acutely aware of the sulfur escaping the boiling cauldrons underground, and suddenly my nausea returns, worse than usual. Fresh replacements are in small, unusually quiet clusters. I approach the first group, where a corpsman is bending over a prone figure. The marines make room for me, and the corpsman looks up and shakes his head. "He's gone."

I don't know how I know, but before I force myself to kneel and look into that face, I am certain he is the kid from Texas. A gaping hole right through the forehead. This is the first time most of these men have seen one of their comrades killed. Their eyes are on me, asking for something, anything, to explain the unexplainable.

I murmur to the corpsman, "Let's get him out of here." I stand up and tell the corporal, "Have a couple of men take him back there. I'll send bearers to carry him away. Then put your men back in single file." As I stand up, I see my pack of cigarettes protruding from the bloody jacket's top pocket.

I hurry down the trail, and as soon as I can find a relatively secluded spot, I veer off from the path and begin to vomit and retch. Beyond the horrors I have witnessed and endured, and beyond the recent deaths of many whom I have come to know and love, this random, ephemeral encounter with the young marine accentuates the fragility of it all. It is a sudden realization, perhaps more piercing because of the arousal of hope I was experiencing an hour ago. Now, in a split second of obliteration, I have an overwhelming, intensely vivid glimpse of impermanence.

I have been oblivious to the activities above me on Mount Suribachi, but I am startled out of my meditation by the incongruous shouts, in Japanese, from a band of marines around the rim of the volcano, seeking to induce enemy troops to surrender. Instinctively, anticipating a response of knee-mortar shells from the bowels of Suribachi rather than capitulation on the part of the Japanese soldiers, I stand up and gather my gear. With the same skepticism, the demolition team is already moving to the crest.

I wind my way, as directly as possible, down the side of the mountain and pick up an easier path about halfway down. Suddenly from above I hear the muffled cracks of what might be Japanese rifle fire inside the volcano. Soon there are the obligatory yells from the demolitions squad, "Fire in the hole! Fire in the hole!" The explosives follow.

I don't look back as I continue down Suribachi. I focus ahead on our tanks crawling into the LST that will carry me away, but peripherally I am assailed by a montage of white crosses and stars, tank hulks, and damaged Superfortresses seeking sanctuary, all interspersed with fleeting images of a bound, writhing Prometheus, the Firebringer—and a beautiful woman grazing my lips with her fingers.

Afterword—and a Love Story

Nature is not so much her own ever-sweet interpreter, as the mere supplier of that cunning alphabet, whereby selecting and combining as he pleases, each man reads his own peculiar lesson according to his own peculiar mind and mood.

Herman Melville, *Pierre; or, The Ambiguities*

Toward the end of World War II, in the winter of 1945, two momentous events took place simultaneously at distant parts of the earth. It can be safely assumed that none of the participants in either of these grim dramas had the remotest knowledge of the others' existence. In southern Poland, the army of the Soviet Union had finished evacuating the German concentration camp of Auschwitz. In the Pacific Ocean, 800 miles south of Japan, three United States Marine divisions were commencing the invasion stage of one of the bloodiest campaigns ever fought, the battle for the island of Iwo Jima, which would be of critical importance as a way station for the flight carrying the first atomic bomb.

William Styron, "The Enduring Metaphors of Auschwitz and Hiroshima," *Newsweek,* January 1993

While I can agree with Styron's choices for enduring metaphors of our times, I hope this memoir serves to excise the Battle of Iwo Jima from such a direct and automatic association with that emblematic event of human suffering, Hiroshima. It is because the metaphors are so powerful and compelling that I seek this exculpation. The survivors of Iwo must be forgiven a hypersensitivity to anything that might diminish those days of uncommon valor. We were, of course, not aware that we were establishing a way station for the first atomic bomb. We appreciated the critical importance of that campaign for the defeat of the Japanese empire, which we anticipated as the eventual outcome of a costly, ferocious invasion of Japan. The atomic bomb introduced a dimension of Prometheus's "all-fashioning fire" far beyond our imagination. As we slide down the slope of advanced technology, this intensification of destructive capacity makes a horrifying difference in the nature of warfare. It is for history to judge when that difference demands that moral choices and alternative strategies be considered.

The young men involved in the events that I have described never considered themselves brave or extraordinary. They were just clear in their minds about who they were and what they were supposed to do as their nation responded to aggressive, fanatical fascism. If that clarity of purpose generated heartfelt camaraderie that soared into heroism, it is a validation of William James's observation that "all of the qualities of a man acquire dignity when he knows that the service of the collectivity that owns him needs them. If proud of the collectivity, his own pride rises in proportion." James's point, of course, is that—so far—war has been the only force that has evoked these qualities.

I have chosen to frame the events of that harrowing month, with less subtlety than I wished, in the context of the myth of Prometheus, the Titan who stole fire from Olympus and gave it to humankind in defiance of Zeus. In revenge Zeus chained Prometheus to a rock, where a vulture continually tore at his liver, until—in the Greek rendition—Prometheus was rescued by Hercules.

In my telling, the compassionate Titan has not yet been rescued. He is forced to witness the frightening folly that human beings are choosing to make of his gift of fire/technology, and Iwo is one of the more horrifying acts in this recurring drama. It was my fate—in 1945, on that sulfurous, volcanic protrusion—for myth and reality to join and present to my mind an enduring metaphor.

But Prometheus is eventually rescued. The myth contains seeds of hope to be strewn on the fallow ground of humankind's future. History is not merely the story of technology writ bold. It reflects also the evolution of thought. Over time, there are more and more fragments of wisdom available to show us how to set free our benefactor Prometheus, to let us recognize and appreciate the collectivity—humanity—that really owns us and to help us attain the wholeness that we lack.

I have looked back from the distance of more than half a century and reflected on a quest that, for me, began in earnest on a July day while we were storming ashore on the island of Guam. It is a journey reviewed through a prism of thoughts borrowed of the wise. It is a journey inspired profoundly by the company of truly brave men and the love of a beautiful woman.

Erna died unexpectedly in 1977, six weeks after being diagnosed with a glioblastoma, a brain cancer. But it was not before we had fulfilled much of our dream, including raising a family of three wonderful children—and not before she helped me resolve a persistent metaphysical enigma.

The profound spiritual challenge for humanity today is the same as always: to experience day by day, event by event, relation by relation, communion between the particular (the *I*) and other particulars (the *Thou*), with perhaps occasionally a glimpse through to what Martin Buber, William James, and others have all named the Eternal Thou. Wrestling with this challenge during some very busy years after the war, I stumbled across an enlightening allegory while browsing through volumes of esoterica in a small bookstore in Manhattan. I could not wait to share this with Erna. Back in the hotel she sensed my excitement and sat down expectantly to hear me relate my tale.

Once upon a time, in ancient India, lived a young, handsome Brahmin's son who was no stranger to the pleasures of the flesh or the intellect. Although many young women of the village were responsive to his slightest attention, he was infatuated with a particularly beautiful, intelligent woman who seemed oblivious to his interest in her.

One evening, after many serious but futile overtures, he knocked at the gates of her home. "Who is there?" she asked.

"It is I," he replied, knowing that she recognized his voice.

The gates did not open, and nothing further was said. Finally he departed and spent many days and nights in deep contemplation of further approaches. After a seemingly interminable period he returned and again knocked at the gates.

"Who is there?" she asked.

"It is Thou," he replied. The gates opened, and they formed an idyllic, loving relationship.

Forever after, he applied this approach to everything in life, offering himself selflessly in all his encounters. According to the legend, after several incarnations he reached a stage where he felt prepared to knock on the gates of heaven. "Who is there?" came the query.

"It is Thou," he confidently replied. The gates did not open.

After some eons of contemplation, he returned and again knocked at the heavenly gates. And again he was asked, "Who is there?"

"It is I," he replied. The gates swung open.

Erna was silent as I searched her face for some reaction. It was a long silence—vexing and reminiscent of Quentin Joy. Finally she remarked, simply, "Yes." Then she smiled and offered, "And it goes down much more easily than Tagore or Schopenhauer."

I relaxed. She came over and, touching my lips softly with her fingers, whispered, "I think you should write about this."

Index

ABOUT THE AUTHOR

Bert Yaffe was born in Sparta, Georgia, and graduated from Emory University in Atlanta. He attended Emory Law School until joining the United States Marine Corps in 1941. Yaffe served in the Pacific for twenty-seven months and was awarded the Purple Heart and two Bronze Stars during the battles of Bougainville, Guam, and Iwo Jima. He achieved the rank of Major.

Yaffe is president of the Yaffe Foundation, chair of the New England Coalition for Health Promotion and Disease Prevention (NECON), and has been internationally recognized for his disease prevention activities.

Bert and his first wife, Erna, had three children before she died of brain cancer in 1977. He and his present wife, Sybil, live in Stockbridge, Massachusetts, and Providence, Rhode Island.

THE NAVAL INSTITUTE PRESS is the book-publishing arm of the U.S. Naval Institute, a private, nonprofit, membership society for sea service professionals and others who share an interest in naval and maritime affairs. Established in 1873 at the U.S. Naval Academy in Annapolis, Maryland, where its offices remain today, the Naval Institute has members worldwide.

Members of the Naval Institute support the education programs of the society and receive the influential monthly magazine Proceedings and discounts on fine nautical prints and on ship and aircraft photos. They also have access to the transcripts of the Institute's Oral History Program and get discounted admission to any of the Institute-sponsored seminars offered around the country.

The Naval Institute also publishes *Naval History* magazine. This colorful bimonthly is filled with entertaining and thought-provoking articles, first-person reminiscences, and dramatic art and photography. Members receive a discount on *Naval History* subscriptions.

The Naval Institute's book-publishing program, begun in 1898 with basic guides to naval practices, has broadened its scope in recent years to include books of more general interest. Now the Naval Institute Press publishes about 100 titles each year, ranging from how-to books on boating and navigation to battle histories, biographies, ship and aircraft guides, and novels. Institute members receive discounts of 20 to 50 percent on the Press's nearly 600 books in print.

Full-time students are eligible for special half-price membership rates. Life memberships are also available.

For a free catalog describing Naval Institute Press books currently available, and for further information about subscribing to *Naval History* magazine or about joining the U.S. Naval Institute, please write to:

Membership Department
U.S. NAVAL INSTITUTE
291 Wood Road
Annapolis, MD 21402-5035
Telephone: (800) 233-8764
Fax: (410) 269-7940
Web address: www.usni.org